# SURREY

IN THE SEVENTIES

## Photographs and memories of the 1970s

*by Mark Davison and Ian Currie*

*Surrey saw some spectacular sights as the Swinging Sixties gave way to the Seventies. Some town centres changed beyond recognition as demolition workers made way for the new, and on the streets, out came some strange new fashions—hot pants, loons, flared trousers, ponchos and platform shoes. As youngsters danced to the Bay City Rollers, Slade and Gary Glitter, the local cinemas were emptying and closing down. The Seventies was also a decade of protests, strikes and other forms of industrial unrest, culminating in the "Winter of Discontent" in 1978-9. The following pages look again at the Seventies in Surrey and recapture those times of happiness and sorrow, Ford Capris, Austin Allegros and Morris Marinas.*

*Students from Winston Churchill School, Woking — wearing platform-soled shoes — attending an interesting lecture about the National Savings Bank, on 4th March 1975.*

**ISBN 0-9516710-7-3 First edition November 1995**

© **Frosted Earth**

Published by *Frosted Earth, 77 Rickman Hill, Coulsdon, Surrey CR5 3DT Tel. 01737 554869*

**Set in 10pt New Century Schoolbook**

Typesetting and design by *Pollyphonics, Roman Way, Farnham, Surrey GU9 9RF*

Printed by *Litho Techniques (Kenley) Ltd., 46-50 Godstone Road, Whyteleafe, Surrey CR3 OEA*

# Acknowledgements

*David Tippett-Wilson, Hook; Tim Everson and the staff at Kingston Heritage Centre; Paul Adams, Long Ditton; Sheila, Colin and Nigel Prendergast; Sutton Herald series; Epsom and Banstead Herald series; London Borough of Croydon Local Studies and Archives staff; Purley Library staff; London Borough of Sutton Heritage Service staff; Museum of Farnham; Farnham Herald series; Jean and Ted Parratt; Woking News and Mail; John Elms for his recollections and pictures of the Leatherhead Golf Course murder case; Keith Walter; the late Ron Poore; Neil McGinn; A.Cattermole for Bookham memories; Maureen Lewington; Greta Morley, editor of both the Dorking Advertiser and Leatherhead Advertiser; Will Stengel, group editor, Surrey and South London Newspapers; Adrian Riches for additional West Surrey research; Fred Coombe and family for guided tour of former Strawberry Studios, Dorking; DJ Mike Read; Jonathan King; Surrey Advertiser photographic staff; Stuart Vaughan; Gladys Arlett and Dorking Museum staff; Z.Miller and the Dorking Pilgrims; The Yicken, Dave and Lorraine Evans for the food and thought; M.and N. Davison, Hook; Susan and Nigel Davison, for anecdotes; Francis Xavier, Dorking; Donald Macphail for Horley snippets; Barry Dix, for Staines air crash recollections; June Sampson; Surrey Local Studies Library, Guildford; John Janaway and colleagues; Kevin Gillen; Geoffrey Godbert, Central Office of Information, Reg Siddons' daughter, Pam; Martin West.*

# Photograph credits

*David Tippett-Wilson of Hook (Esher bypass protest; cubs' football at Tolworth; Sainsbury's at Hook; firemen in mud; Churchfields protest; Tory canvassers in Hook and Surbiton; stars at Tolworth; 281 bus; Surbiton demolition pictures; Surbiton Odeon; Malden Underpass' first traffic and crowd; Kingston aerial and town centre pictures and demolition of Brady's Arcade; Harry Secombe; Kingston Carnival float and for access to his archives from Kingston Borough News); Surrey Advertiser (Guildford scenes; Brookwood girls, Cranleigh children and Godalming youth; Ranmore teenager; Forest Green crash; Frimley Park Hospital); Deniz Corday (Walton Hop collection); Surrey Comet (Reg Siddons at Kingston and arrest at Malden Underpass); Adrian Boot (Boomtown Rats); Iain Wakeford of Old Woking for the Woking photographic archives; Richmond-upon-Thames public library local studies section; Richmond and Twickenham Times (Richmond Borough pictures); London Borough of Sutton Heritage Service's Archives and Local Studies Section (Sutton scenes); London Borough of Croydon Local Studies and Archives Service (Croydon scenes originating from the Croydon Advertiser Group Ltd.); Mr M.Scott (High Street) and the Croydon Natural History and Scientific Society (metric protest); London Borough of Croydon, Purley Library (Purley street scenes and college); Surrey Mirror series' archives (street scenes in Redhill, Reigate, Oxted and Horley, The Star, Hooley, M25 opening and pre-opening, Sybil Star, Redhill fires, hospital campaign, Caterham bombing); Dorking and Leatherhead Advertiser series (Leatherhead murder case, shop advertisements, Embassy); Elmbridge Borough Council's Weybridge Museum (Elmbridge street scenes); Epsom and Ewell Borough Council, Bourne Hall Museum (Epsom and Ewell street scenes plus Status Quo advert, East Ewell Station and Glyn Arms public house, Ewell launderette); Anne Jones, Museum of Farnham; Farnham and Haslemere scenes accessed from Farnham Herald archives; Dorking Museum (Dorking High Street, Wheatsheaf, Romano coffee shop); Rykas, Box Hill (Rykas burger bar); Dave Shiers (access to Dorking disco and motorbike pictures by Xavier); Fred Coombes and family (Strawberry Studios archives); Jack Underwood (Surrey Mirror promotional material 1970s); Charlie Whiting (punk teenager); Ian Allan and pals (Leatherhead boys meet The Police); Mark Davison collection (Esher bypass horse protest, Hook Road; Hook buses and ticket; Smelly Nellie; lollipop lady; Surbiton fire station and crew; Kingston murders; Norman Lamont; Banstead material; Walton reservoir; Donny Osmond); Malcolm Pendrill FBIPP, FRPS, FRSA (Reigate Christmas scene); Angela Burden, Surrey Herald archives (Staines air crash). Hook flood picture, Mr Webber. Godalming: Christmas scene, Ron Head; High Street scene, Alan High; other pictures: Surrey Advertiser; Adela Goodall, Godalming Museum.*

***Special thanks to:** David Tippett-Wilson of Hook for access to his extensive photographic archives of Hook and the rest of the Royal Borough of Kingston, collected over many years; Terry Habgood of the Surrey Advertiser photographic team; Graham Collyer, editor of the Surrey Advertiser; Neil White and all the helpful staff of Weybridge Museum; Jennie Currie; Iain Wakeford for his extensive contribution to the Woking section; Richmond Borough local studies library, at Richmond, for their patience and understanding; Jeremy Harte, dedicated curator of the Bourne Hall Museum.*

***Front cover design:** Mark Davison, Sue Attwood plus Dave and Roger Swan of Woodend Studios, Beare Green, Surrey.*

***Frosted Earth logo:** Cathie Shuttleworth*

# Bibliography

*The Amber Valley Gazeteer of Greater London's Suburban Cinemas 1946-86 by Malcolm Webb; British Hit Singles series (Guinness); Top 40 Charts (Guinness); Surrey Comet series; Surrey Mirror series; Woking Review; Woking News and Mail series; Surrey Advertiser series; Dorking and Leatherhead Advertiser series; Richmond and Twickenham Times; Sutton, Epsom and Banstead Herald series; Farnham Castle Newspapers; Surrey Herald series; Croydon Advertiser group; Kingston Borough News archives; Bob Geldof, Is That It (Sidgwick and Jackson 1986); Rock Gazeteer of Great Britain, compiled by Pete Frame (Banyan Books 1989).*

Flares were all the fashion in 1975 — the wider, the trendier. Here, young pop songwriter Barry Rice, who lived at Ranmore Common, near Dorking, can be seen wearing platform shoes, which were also in vogue. His tee-shirt carries an artist's impression of Steve Harley, who had a number one hit in February 1975, with '(Come up and See Me) Make me Smile,' from his band Cockney Rebel.

Above left: youngsters and adults joined the protest about the building of the Esher bypass. This demonstration was held in Woodstock Lane, Claygate, on Saturday 22nd June 1974. Above right: the "Chessington Kid" joins dozens of horse riders in the demonstration. They are pictured in Woodstock Lane, Claygate.

Above, left: leading bypass protestor, Mrs Mollie Worthy, puts up a campaign poster in Claygate, following the horseback demonstration in June 1974. Above, right: a public meeting is staged in Hook, to try and halt the proposed bypass. On the left of the picture is Mollie Worthy, taking notes. Second from right is action group member John McMeechan, who lived in Claremont Road, Surbiton.

Even though it had been proposed as long ago as the 1930s, when detailed plans were drawn up to construct a six-lane bypass for Esher, in 1974 there was an outcry from villagers in Claygate, Chessington and Hook. They were outraged at the prospect of seeing the motorway-style road, which would cost £10.5 million, tear up their playing fields, commons and woods.

An action group was formed following a stormy meeting at Hook Community Centre in 1974. Leading the campaign was Mollie Worthy, of Bramham Gardens, Hook, a mother in her late forties, who had turned "green" in a big way. She had a shield on the front of her bicycle which read: "Bring back the bicycle to beautiful Britain." People of all ages joined the protest. Letters were sent to the Queen and to the Prime Minister, Harold Wilson, but to no avail.

In October 1974, three of the greatest opponents of the new bypass, Tom Fahy, Peter Garrow and John McMeechan, travelled to Grimsby and hunted down Environment Secretary Tony Crosland. He agreed to meet them and seemed surprised at their determination.

On another occasion, protestors ripped up perimeter fences around the bypass route at Hook, and there were reports of contractors' bulldozers being sabotaged at night.

W.C.French, the contractors, completed the road in December 1976 — three months early.

# Esher bypass protest

Mollie Worthy, a leading campaigner against the Esher bypass, had to admit defeat when it opened, three months ahead of schedule, on Wednesday 15th December 1976. Police removed the barriers at 11.17am, but there was no grand ceremony. Representatives of the contractors, W.C. French, plus officers from the Department of the Environment watched as the barriers were removed. The £10.5 million six-lane highway cut through the green fields behind Hook, Chessington and Claygate and there had been furious protests in a bid to get the road-building stopped. However, it was all to no avail and the bypass formed a new section of the A3 London to Portsmouth trunk road.

Above: final touches are made to the start of the new Esher bypass west of Hook Underpass. Right: the contractors, W.C. French, boast that completion is three months ahead of schedule.

The fight is lost. Mollie Worthy was the sole protestor present on the day that the Esher bypass was opened. She is seen chatting forlornly to Hook's beat bobby, PC Eric Blumfield.

*Dittons, Hinchley Wood, Molesey, Esher, Claygate*

# Elmbridge in 1976

Long-haired teenager, Peter Lowman, of Brooklands Technical College, was the first to make the news in 1976 when he was voted one of the best engineering students to be taken on by the Post Office.

At about the same time, other successes were being celebrated. The Esher Youth Theatre staged two polished performances of "Life of the Insects" at Claygate Village Hall, and the Hinchley Manor Operatic Society clocked up its 100th performance when it gave a show to Chessington over-60s. Also at Claygate Village Hall, the local dramatic society performed Aladdin and in Elizabeth White: "Claygate had a splendid Aladdin who could sing, act and strut around in the principal boy tradition," wrote Hinchley Wood show critic Peter Tatlow.

Claygate's Albert "Dixie" Dean was also in the news in January 1976. As lettings secretary of the Claygate Village Hall, he was praised by villagers for the tremendous success of the busy hall and was presented with a portrait of himself, painted by Thomas Edwards, of The Roundway, Claygate.

Not so happy at that time was Esher's MP, Carol Mather, and his constituents in Molesey who were incensed about aircraft noise and urged him to write to the Department of Trade, seeking compensation.

A more pleasant noise could be heard at The Foley Arms, Claygate, where the Thames Valley Morris Men often played and danced, or at Ye Olde Swan, Thames Ditton, where the Fiddlers Green band provided entertainment.

Fears for the Sunday service at Thames Ditton station grew early in 1976, but the weekday service was busy, with 554 commuters using Thames Ditton and 1,213 travelling from Hampton Court.

After work, some may have relaxed in The Embassy, Esher, watching films such as the X-rated Dog Day Afternoon. At Walton Odeon, in the same week, Jungle Book and The Return of the Big Cat were being screened.

Tragedy struck in Claygate, days after the death of Violet Phillips at The Lodge, Stevens Lane. A fire broke out at Foxwarren, killing three-year-old Lee Challis.

Thames Ditton had a new vicar early in 1976. He was the Reverend Paul Conder, of Merseyside, who came to the parish with his wife, Lesley. She was reported to be keen on fencing and was looking for a club to join.

The UCS chain, with a branch at 55, Walton Road, East Molesey, advertised second-hand cars. A 1973 Morris Marina ("white, lovely condition") was offered for £795.

A 1974 Hillman Hunter GLS ("sandalwood, vinyl roof") was £545 and a three-year-old Ford Escort 1100 ("blue, roomy, economic car") was advertised for £785.

In Hare Lane, Claygate, builders nearing completion of The Firs flats for elderly people celebrated with a topping-out ceremony. Perhaps it was time to go to a gala night at The White Lodge Taverna in Creek Road, East Molesey where, on 6th February 1976, entertainment was provided by Aphrodite (Love Goddess).

Less content were ratepayers in Hinchley Wood, who staged a protest in the shopping parade against the rate increases in Elmbridge. They collected 1,300 signatures during February.

Unhappy, too, were hundreds of Weston Green residents, who suffered several hours of power cuts in the same month, which meant TV sets were blacked out. On BBC 1 Kojak, Doctor Who (starring Tom Fox), Look—Mike Yarwood, plus It's Cliff and Friends were all showing at the time. On ITV Sale of The Century, with Nicholas Parsons was being broadcast mid-evening. Youngsters escaping this family viewing decided to head for the weekly disco at the Walton Hop or make for a show by The Troggs, at the College of Food Technology in Weybridge.

The Odeon, Walton was showing Window to The Sky (A) in February 1976, but if you couldn't sit still for that long, you could dance to the Shuffle Sisters at The Walton Hop on 5th March or The Curfew Stompers at the Thames Hotel, Hampton Court, a week later.

Comedian Michael Bentine, who lived in Esher, presented five portable TV sets to the rehabilitation camp at RAF Chessington in early March.

Masked raiders struck at Long Ditton Post Office, Winter's Bridge, during a rainstorm on 12th March. Sub-postmaster Edward Davies told police he had been coshed over the head. Nearly £2,000 was stolen.

*'Britain's first disco'*

# The Walton Hop

**Happy Hop members, at Walton, in the late Seventies.**

The Walton Hop is claimed to be Britain's first discotheque and it was here that thousands of teenagers gathered, in the Seventies, to hear their favourite pop groups. The Bay City Rollers were among those who performed to adoring fans at the Hop, held every week in The Playhouse, Walton.

For 32 years, from 1958-1990, the Hop brought happiness to young people. It turned out to be one of the longest-running discos in the world.

It was started by Deniz Corday, originally from Bermuda, who, as a youngster in 1956, was keen to get into film direction work. A film company offered him a trip to Shepperton Studios and from that point the Walton link grew.

He worked in the record department of Birkhead's in Church Street, Walton, and soon realized that youngsters wanted to listen to rock and roll music, which they could not hear on BBC radio. He started the Hop so that teenagers could have somewhere to dance to this new style of music. On 3rd June, 1958, the first 'Hop' dance was held.

Its popularity grew and grew and it was not just teenagers who flocked to the venue from all over the South East. The Sixties got into full swing and, throughout the decade, it was the favourite Friday nightspot to meet like-minded young men and women.

The 1970s were, arguably, the heyday of the Hop. Excellent resident DJs pulled in the crowds, up-and-coming bands performed, there were spec-

Jonathan King—Surrey's enterprising pop star, who made visits to The Hop as a guest DJ.

Deniz Corday, The Hop's founder, who provided entertainment for Surrey's youngsters for 32 years.

Bay City Rollers—the Seventies' group who made two appearances at The Hop.

DENIZ CORDAY
proudly presents

★ OUR 19th ★
BIRTHDAY
★ PARTY ★
HOP
SPECIAL
★ THIS ★
SATURDAY
★ 10th Sept. ★

Don't miss this really great party nite, when we will be celebrating 19 years of happy Hop dancing Featuring all our

★ Party Specials ★
★ including ★
Special Party
★ Dances ★
Streamers
Balloons
Coke Drinking
★ Contests ★
Mummy Wrapping

PLAYHOUSE
THE
WALTON
HOP
DISCOTHEQUE
★ ★ CLUB ★ ★
CATERING FOR HAPPY
YOUNG    PEOPLE
BETWEEN
★ 14 and 21 ★
NOW IN OUR 20th
YEAR — AND STILL THE
BIGGEST AND THE BEST
COME AND SEE FOR
★ YOURSELF ★

WITH
★ D.J.s RICKI ★
★ & FRANKIE ★

★ EVERY ★
FRIDAY
★ 'SPECIAL ★
LIVE GROUP SPOT
OPEN 7.30, 7.45-11.30
ADM. 50p

★ EVERY ★
SATURDAY
★ SPECIAL ★
HOP MIMERS
OPEN 7.30, 8-12

An advertisement for the Walton Hop in 1977.

tacular party nights and mummy-wrapping events. Sometimes small groups of youths scuffled outside the venue but there was never any trouble inside.

Vital to the success of The Hop were the many resident DJs. Among these were brothers, Rikki and Frankie Forte, who came from Ghana, Vince Lee and David Underhill. Famous singer and songwriter, Jonathan King, often deejayed at The Hop for no charge. He was a good friend of Deniz Corday, and respected The Hop's professional management.

Mike Read, of BBC radio and TV, was also a guest DJ, as was Jimmy Pursey of Sham 69 pop group. Rob Randall and Chris Denning were also seen behind the turntable on occasions.

In the 1970s, Deniz Corday started showing cartoon films projected on the walls. He then began showing film footage, that he had taken of events such as performances in the latter part of the Seventies by Rosetta Stone and Streetboy. Hop members were excited at seeing themselves on film.

Miming to pop groups in the charts was a feature of The Hop. Mimers took their preparation work seriously and made special outfits, rehearsed their routines and put on make-up. Local acts used miming at The Hop as a way to get noticed by 'big-wigs' in the industry. Jimmy Pursey and the Ferrets mimed to the Bay City Rollers and later became the successful punk band Sham 69, giving one show, under that name, at The Hop.

One ex-Hop member, Kathy Gibbons, later recalled that, in 1977, she and friends wore long black dresses while miming to "Yes Sir, I Can Boogie," by Baccara. They had studied what Baccara members were wearing for the song's film on Top of the Pops. The reward for performers was two free tickets to

**A fun night out at the Walton Hop in the late 1970s.**

The Hop.

St. Valentine's night and New Year's Eve, were very special party nights at The Hop. The hall would have up to 300 balloons hanging from the ceiling for the Valentine's party. The "Hokey-Cokey," "Simon Says" and the Conga routines were firm favourites on New Year's Eve.

Blind dates were arranged on other occasions, when a pair would set off for the cinema. Long-term relationships sometimes followed and there were even a couple of marriages.

Rock and roll went out of fashion, with the skinheads, in the early 1970s and the DJs started playing reggae. Desmond Dekker's "You Can Get It If You Really Want," Dave and Ansil Collins' "Double Barrel," and Horace Faith's "Black Pearl" were all in the charts around this time.

Deniz later recalled: "When the skinhead scene started to come in slowly, we had to begin playing reggae music, which the rockers didn't like."

The Bay City Rollers premiered at The Hop in 1971 and, four years later, made a surprise appearance at the venue again. They asked the crowd what should be their new single and tried out some songs. The verdict? "Bye Bye Baby!" Their manager, Tom Paton, also had another group under his wing, called Rosetta Stone, which he premiered at the Hop in 1977.

The late '70s punk music was not played because it was difficult to dance to.

Mummy-wrapping was a bizarre, but fun, form of entertainment and was enormously popular. People would get up on stage and be wrapped in toilet paper to look like a mummy. This was done whilst a record was played. When the record had finished the crowd had to judge who was the most convincing-looking mummy. Then the contestants burst out of their wrapping.

Ricki Forte was a regular DJ at the club.

Jimmy Pursey, a Hersham boy and member of Sham 69, occasionally played records at The Hop.

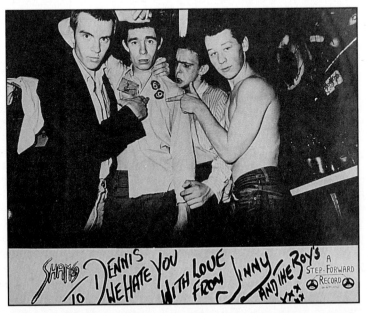

Radio One DJ, Mike Read, sometimes visited The Hop. Here he is handing out singles at the club's 21st anniversary, in September 1979.

A fond greeting, written in jest, from Hersham punk band Sham 69, to Deniz Corday.

# Cliff in Walton, the Two Ronnies in Claygate

Singer Cliff Richard marked the 21st anniversary, on 5th October 1976, of Walton's Pet Shop by presenting budgerigars to local pensioners. Cliff, who arrived from his home in St. George's Hill, bought food for his dog at the shop. Among the recipients of the caged birds were Mrs Jennie Andrews, who lived in St. Helen's, Weston Green, and Mr Arthur Woodcraft, whose home was in Dunstable Road, Molesey.

Residents in a quiet Claygate street looked out of their windows in disbelief, on 12th May 1976, when they saw TV comedian, Ronnie Corbett, cycling by in shorts and hurling daily newspapers over their garden fences. He and Ronnie Barker, The Two Ronnies, were in Coverts Road, near the Foxwarren, for two days, being filmed for their new BBC series to be shown in the autumn of 1976. Wearing a faded blue tee-shirt and denim jeans, the assistant producer of the show, Marcus Plantin, of Avenue Elmers, Surbiton, said he and the producer, Terry Hughes, who lived in Queen's Road, Kingston, chose Claygate for the filming because "it is a pretty little village."

The Esher May Queen, and her attendants, at the Esher May Fair in 1975.

The now-vanished Three Pigeons public house in Portsmouth Road, Long Ditton, in 1978.

The 218 RF bus in Hersham Road in 1974.

Weybridge town centre in the Seventies.

Looking west along Weybridge High Street, on 26th March 1974.

The Queen Mother opens the new grandstand at Sandown Racecourse, Esher, on 22nd September 1973.

*Old lady lived in a house full of milk bottles*

# Tragedy of 'Smelly Nellie'

**Left: The Lodge, in Claygate, where Miss Phillips lived in squalor, with no gas or electricity.**

**Right: Violet Phillips, as a young woman. Later she was to live in appalling conditions in the heart of a wealthy Surrey village.**

Firemen, called to a fire in a wealthy part of Claygate, in the small hours of Sunday, 4th January, 1976, were in for a shock. Inside The Lodge, Stevens Lane, they found the body of an elderly recluse, who had been living in astonishing conditions. The rooms were several feet deep in milk bottles and rubbish and, to get around, channels and tunnels had been made through the litter. There was no water, no electricity and no gas, and the windows were boarded up. Miss Violet Phillips, aged 78, had just a transistor radio for company and read by the light of candles. She was unknown to Elmbridge Council's Social Services.

Her body was found buried under three feet of rubbish in the hovel. It was only after firemen had been called back to The Lodge, near Ruxley Towers, that the grim discovery was made. They had presumed the premises were derelict. Neighbours summoned the brigade when the rubbish started smouldering again. On forking it over they found Miss Phillips.

Despite her strange life-style, neighbours recalled that Miss Phillips was a well-educated and well-spoken woman. She had lived at The Lodge since the 1930s. Her niece, Mrs Pamela Guest, of Frome, Somerset, told an inquest in Epsom that her aunt had lived alone in the house since 1939. She had not allowed any member of the family to go inside her home and was something of an eccentric recluse. It was thought the fire had been started by a naked candle flame igniting rubbish, or heat from a methylated spirit stove setting fire to junk, the coroner heard.

The Fire Brigade's Sub Officer Jon Dixon, said it would have been extremely difficult for Miss Phillips to have escaped from the house, because of the rubbish. An open verdict was recorded.

Miss Phillips, known affectionately as Smelly Nellie, was a gardener in Esher, until the age of 76. One of her employees, Mrs Vera Boote, of The Lodge, Lower Green Road, Esher, later told the *Kingston Borough News*: "She was an absolutely amazing woman - most extraordinary. She told me her father was a doctor, near Montague Square, London, and that her grandmother lived in Scotland. Once, when she was gardening, I noticed she had burnt her arm on the paraffin stove which she cooked on, so I bathed it in pure honey. It was only in the latter days she let things get like they did. It was not like that when I lived at Ruxley in 1941."

Miss Phillips was said to have been friendly with an Alice Christmas, who lived near Esher Green and whose home had also fallen into disrepair.

**One of the rooms in The Lodge, where Miss Phillips lived. It was waist-deep in milk bottles. She made tunnels through the debris so that she could get around in her home.**

**These West Surrey squatters had their own accommodation problems, in March 1975, but managed to keep warm, despite the chilly Easter weather, by drinking mugs of hot tea. A photographer from the *Surrey Advertiser*, in Guildford, paid them a visit on 24th March.**

*Thames Ditton traders up in arms over yellow lines*

# Cutbacks on the buses

In April 1976, London Transport announced cutbacks in the bus service. Fewer journeys would be made on the 218 (Kingston-Esher-Staines), on the 219 (Kingston-Esher-Weybridge), the 211 (Kingston-Molesey-Walton), and on the 264 (Kingston-Sunbury-Walton-Hersham Green). Hinchley Wood was to lose its 189 service from Hook, which originated at Clapham Common. Claygate also feared further cutbacks to the 206 service.

In the same month, Claygate villagers protested that too many lorries involved in the Esher bypass construction were using local roads, and there was drama in Claygate on Wednesday 7th April, when a homemade bomb was found under a car in Telegraph Lane.

A man died in an horrific accident on the Kingston bypass, near Woodstock Lane, Long Ditton.

The accident involved two cars — a Ford Cortina and a Daimler.

Thames Ditton traders were up in arms over plans to introduce double yellow lines outside their shops. In nearby Long Ditton, people were upset that W.G.Furnish, in Thorkhill Road, announced its closure after some 80 years, following the retirement of Mr William Furnish.

The other branches of Furnish in Summer Road, Thames Ditton; Ditton Hill; Ewell Road, Surbiton and at Ham, were set to continue under new owners.

Thames Ditton residents were also disquieted by aircraft noise and complained that, instead of sitting out in their gardens enjoying the good weather, they were forced to stay indoors with their French windows shut tight.

A VIP made a visit to the area. Piloting a bright red Wessex helicopter of the Queen's flight, Prince Philip landed in the drizzle at Sandown Racecourse, on Wednesday 12th May, for the start of an informal visit to two Esher factories — Redwood Burn Ltd. and James Burn Binding Ltd.

His main host that morning was Mr David Gieve, OBE, chairman of both companies. Ten million books were bound, annually, at Redwood Burn.

As the 1976 drought became more acute, residents of Weston Green feared for Marney's Pond, which by the middle of May could be walked across without people getting their feet wet.

To celebrate the 21st anniversary of the Horse Rangers at Hampton Court, Princess Margaret made a special visit in early June.

## The hermit in the woods at Oxshott

**In the Seventies, a recluse lived in the woods between Oxshott and Leatherhead. "Old Ted" Churcher's home for more than 30 years was a tent in the wood**ed Pachesham Park next to Prince's Coverts.

Sometimes he could be seen wheeling a barrow along the Leatherhead Road, near The Star pub.

He proved to be a valuable help to police in 1971 when the Leatherhead Golf Course murder inquiry was launched, because his valuable knowledge of every nook and cranny of the countryside near Pachesham Gate, helped police find the body.

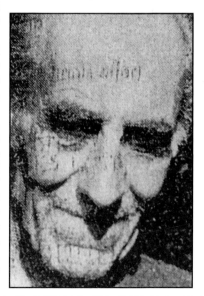

Popular lollipop lady, Mrs Doris Stonard, saw pupils of St. Paul's School, Hook, across the road safely, for 22 years until her sudden death on 19th September, 1976, at the age of 54.. She is pictured here in 1975.

German/Jewish refugee, the late Paul Gordon-Fischel, was a familiar sight in Hook. His remarkable white beard earned him the nickname of Father Christmas. He lived at 230, Hook Road, with his wife, Frances.

An RT 65 bus to Chessington Zoo, makes a stop in Hook Road, Hook, c. 1972. The bus offers 7-day rover tickets for £5.30.

The 2nd Hook 'B' Cubs won 3-0 in the Surbiton and district Cub Scout football finals, held in 1972. The match at the Decca Sports Ground, Tolworth, was settled by goals from Nigel Davison (2), and S. Morris. This win meant Hook completed the 'double,' having already won a league title.

Bill Cole, who was known as "The Chessington Kid," and who lived in Woodgate Avenue, Hook, was a local character. A keen cyclist, he fought the building of the Esher bypass, in 1974-5, appearing at demonstrations and other events.

# Hook and Chessington

It was "all change" on the buses in the Seventies. The 65A service, from Ealing to Chessington Zoo, via Copt Gilders, was replaced by route 65, while 71s ran from Richmond to Leatherhead, replacing the 65 service which covered the main Leatherhead Road. In October, 1975, the RT buses which had served the routes since before the 1950s, were replaced with RM models. Conductors still collected the fares. The best-known conductress was a friendly, outgoing lady called Scottie, from Kingston. She packed the passengers on board with a cheerful smile, even though the bus was full. This picture was taken about 1971, opposite the White Hart, Hook. Note the posters advertising the space-age film, 2001, which was first released in the late 1960s. Prior to 1969, the 65 route went beyond Chessington, to Leatherhead bus garage.

Sainsbury's, Hook, marking the Queen's Jubilee in 1977.

Sainsbury's still offered a counter service at its branch in Ace Parade, Hook, during the 1970s, and pyramids of canned food continued to be displayed in the front window.

Surbiton's firemen were not usually the stick-in-the-mud sort, but on a winter's day in the late Seventies, they got that sinking feeling while driving across Chessington's Churchfields Recreation Ground.

Chessington residents were alarmed by plans to build a council housing estate on Churchfields Recreation Ground in 1975. Surbiton's MP, Sir Nigel Fisher, wished 500 campaigners luck in their fight.

Actor, Michael Balfour, visited a Hook fête event in the Seventies, which was staged next to Hook Parish Hall.

Flared trousers were all the rage when this photograph of Conservative campaigners was taken c.1976, at Arcade Parade, Hook.

Alan is Number One at H[

Alan Freeman, the Radio One DJ, visited Hook Youth Club, Devon Way, Hook, in October 1976, just after the long, hot summer ended.

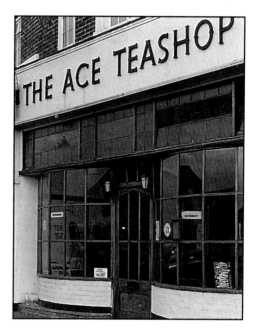

The Ace Teashop, at Ace Parade, Hook, closed in October 1976. It later became a restaurant.

# Stars turn out at Tolworth

Well over 2,000 people flocked to Tolworth to watch a charity soccer extravaganza held on Sunday 28th September 1975, at the Decca Sports Ground. The event, organized by Surbiton Scouts, was in aid of John Edrich's testimonial year. The Surrey and England Cricketers' team, which included several Surrey players, lost by two goals to five to an all-star team captained by Dennis Waterman of TV's The Sweeney and later Minder, with George Cole. For the all-stars, former Arsenal goalkeeper Bob Wilson was said to be in "terrific form" and stole the show, with "two fine goals." Queen's Park Rangers' manager, Dave Sexton, scored from a free-kick and BBC racing correspondent Julian Wilson also found the net. TV's Man About The House actress, Sally Thomsett, who played the part of Jo in the series, kicked off the match. In the picture, from left to right are Scouts organizer Ted Barley, top cricketer John Edrich, Mick Bidmead, Sally Thomsett and the team's captain, Dennis Waterman.

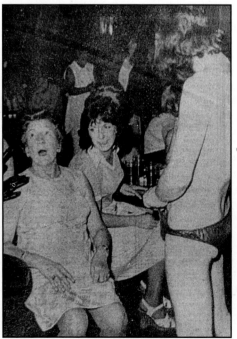

The Toby Jug, at Tolworth, which featured big-name pop groups in the Sixties, offered a new type of entertainment in the mid-Seventies. In July 1976, stripper, Mr X, proved quite revealing at the venue's first-ever hen party. "The women, from teenage girls to middle-aged housewives and mothers, who came from all over Surrey for the show, chanted and cheered as bearded Mr X, dressed in a leather Alvin Stardust-type suit, performed for them," reported the *Kingston Borough News*, adding: "a middle-aged woman with whiting hair and wearing a green checked dress got over-excited and tried to tear away the stripper's G-string, as he paraded through the audience."

An early autumn downpour on Wednesday 22nd September 1976, helped put an end to the summer drought. Here, at Surbiton Crescent, Surbiton, an RM 281 red bus negotiates flood water en route to Kingston, from Tolworth Broadway and Ewell Road. The torrential rain caused the closure of the Hook Underpass, resulting in huge traffic jams back to Tolworth Underpass, where four cars were involved in a collision. More heavy rain followed over the next two days and there was thunder at Hook.

## *Secretaries could earn £2,500 a year*

# Tolworth and Surbiton in 1976

Surbiton was lashed by gales in the first week of January 1976. A chimney crashed through the roof of the Bentalls trainees' hostel at Avenue Elmers and landed in the loft, saving the occupants from serious injury. Trees crashed down in Worthington Road, Tolworth, Chamberlain Way, Surbiton, and at other locations in the Queen of the Suburbs.

It was thought to have been the worst gale since 1947, with winds in London reaching 75mph, leading to widespread damage across the region. There was also another storm in the same week, but in this case a political one. A row blew up over plans to close Berrylands, Tolworth and Chessington North and South stations on winter Sundays. There was another rumpus over proposals by Kingston Council to force Wallaker's estate agents in Tolworth Broadway to take down their

well-known revolving clock because it was "detrimental to the architectural character of the building and the terrace of which it forms part."

In mid-January, controversial pop star Judge Dredd, planned to make a guest appearance at Rob Randall's disco at the Charrington Bowl but meanwhile, a professional theatre company had some very red faces when not a single person turned up at Surbiton Assembly Rooms for their performance of The Hollow Crown. The cast were confronted by rows of 500 empty canvas chairs.

In February, Kingston Council turned down plans by Lambeth and Wandsworth Council to build a housing estate at Tolworth Court Farm.

The well-known Hardwick family, of Eversley Road, Surbiton, launched a petition in February, after Kingston Council refused to let them return to their council house. Earlier, a residents' associ-

**The hot summers of 1975 and 1976 enabled children to have fun at playschemes organized during the school holidays. Here, children from the Surbiton area enjoy one such gathering. In the centre is a young-looking Kingston Labour Councillor, Andrew Mackinlay, who lived at Leatherhead Road, Malden Rushett, and in later years became an MP for Thurrock, in Essex. One of the playschemes, in August 1976, was held on the Alpha Road estate, in Surbiton and involved painting walls and taking part in obstacle races at the nearby Fishponds Park.**

ation in the Addison Gardens area had allegedly petitioned local people in a bid to stop Bill Hardwick and his family from moving back in.

At Bishop's supermarket in Ewell Road, Tolworth, there were several special offers in March 1976. Buxted oven-ready chickens were just 24p per pound and Danela Butter was only 16p for half-a-pound. Ribena was 39p for a family bottle and Quick Brew tea bags were 52p for a box of 144.

Criticism was aimed at Tolworth Girls' School in February 1976, for spending 84p on purchasing a snail for biology lessons. A spokesman for the school said it was essential for research and that there had been a shortage of snails owing to the hot summer of 1975.

Meanwhile, in Victoria Road, Surbiton, Sam Cook's, the fruiterers, gained an award for being the cleanest and most efficient shop out of all the Sam Cook branches. Manager, Mr Maurice Blake, was chuffed —it was the fifth time the store had been presented with the cup.

A Surbiton pensioner, Arthur Tiddy, known as The Chocolate Man of Khatmandu, continued to tour the poor areas of Nepal, handing out confectionery to enfeebled children.

The 69-year-old pensioner had made five visits to Nepal by the spring of 1976 and always returned to his Victorian home in Arlington Road, with fascinating tales.

At the Julian Bengry Motors garage in Browns Road, Surbiton, fashionable cars were on sale. These included the Opel Kadett saloon, The City and The Kadett Coupé, which offered "outstanding road-holding from the highly refined coil spring suspension." The Kadett saloon was praised for offering up to 41 miles per gallon on two-star petrol.

There were fears in April 1976 that 72 council homes in Addison Gardens may be demolished because a ten-year war against cockroaches had still been unsuccessful.

In May, local secretaries could earn up to £2,500 in Tolworth, provided they had excellent shorthand, but the average secretarial salary was just over £2,000, according to advertisements placed by Suburbia Staff Bureau at Winthrop House, St. Mark's Hill.

**Surbiton Fire Station's White Watch crew in September 1978. From left to right: Dick Davies, Steve Matthews, Ken Beale, Nick Fisher, and Charlie Beauchamp. Fireman Matthews was the youngest crew member, at 20 years of age. The station's cook, Mrs Sylvia Bryant, used to enjoy preparing a favourite snack of cheese, onion and Branston Pickle sandwiches for her "boys" but there were occasional groans if the pickle had run out.**

This parade of shops in Brighton Road, Surbiton, was pulled down in the mid-Seventies. Formerly, the line-up of stores included two sweet shops, The Old Bakery and Maypines, the electrical dealers, who sometimes employed youths on Saturdays to hand out leaflets advertising their wares. The firm, which specialized in the repair and sales of monochrome (black and white) television receivers, had a distinctive red and yellow sign above the shop door and a similar logo on the yellow GPO-type van parked outside. Note the poster on the window of the derelict corner shop advertising a concert by Can, a progressive rock group from Germany, at the Civic Hall, Guildford, on Sunday 29th September 1974 and a notice about the Robert Brothers' circus at Epsom, featuring Coco the Clown. The Old Bakery was owned by Mr. J. Humphreys, who also purchased another bakery at Ewell before retiring. He was a keen yachtsman and kept a motor cruiser on the south coast. One of the two sweet shops sold a higher class of confectionery and was run by two "upright citizens" who later retired. The other shop was more for schoolchildren buying small items at 1p each. Opposite this parade of shops was the office of the *Kingston Borough News*, Nuttings the grocery shop and Milo's Café, where puddings included a bowl of sago. Nuttings closed in December 1976 after trading from the same premises for 68 years.

Making way for the new... these Victorian "semis" opposite Christchurch, King Charles Road, Surbiton, were pulled down c.1975.

The Wombles of Wimbledon Common became popular TV characters and had many hit records. Their creator, Mike Batt, lived in Langley Avenue, Surbiton. They made many appearances at Surrey fêtes in 1976. This one was at the New Malden Ambulance Station's 999 Fair, in Wellington Crescent, on 4th September.

Firemen sit around their makeshift shelter at Surbiton Fire Station in late November 1977, during the firemen's pay dispute, which affected the majority of stations in the region. During the crisis, the golf clubhouse in Home Park, near Hampton Court, burnt down and the glow from the fire could be seen from the banks of the Thames at Surbiton.

Surbiton's Conservative MP, Sir Nigel Fisher, campaigns in his constituency for re-selection in 1974. The results in the election: Sir Nigel 15,330;  Andrew Mackinlay (Labour) 9,309; David Brooke (Liberal) 8,931.

Singer Joan Armatrading, who lived close to Surbiton Assembly Rooms, is pictured making a special appearance at Surbiton's MJM record store in Victoria Road, where she signed copies of her latest album, Joan Armatrading, which eventually spent 27 weeks in the charts. The visit was on 12th October 1976. Four days later, her first UK hit single, "Love and Affection," entered the hit parade lists and eventually climbed to number 10.

# Last days of The Odeon

Surbiton's Odeon cinema closed its doors for good on Saturday 8th February 1975, leaving the town with no cinemas, because The Ritz, on St. Mark's Hill, had become a bingo hall after closing as a picture house on 17th May 1966. Rank claimed that the 1,402-seat Odeon had to shut because it was losing so much money. Manager Mr Charles Frith retired on the same day as the closure. Usherette, Mrs Violet Page and kiosk cashier, Mrs Flo Taylor, lost their jobs. Mrs Taylor had worked in the kiosk for 17 years. Mrs Page had been employed at The Odeon, in Claremont Road, Surbiton, since the war. The last film to be shown was Cinderella Liberty (X) and To Kill A Clown. Mrs Page said that too many sex films were being shown and pensioners had been driven away. The Odeon became a D.I.Y. store.

**Severe flooding hit the Hook, Tolworth and Chessington area on Friday evening 6th July 1973, after a rush hour cloudburst. The storm delivered an incredible 4.65 inches of rain in an hour-and-a-half. Three hundred homes were flooded, some to a depth of four feet, causing sofas and pianos to float around living rooms. Fire brigade pumps arrived from as far away as Kent to help with the huge mopping-up operation. At the time it was the 20th heaviest rainstorm ever experienced in the British Isles in a day. This was Hook Road, Hook, near the Ace of Spades.**

# Action in Surbiton

Residents of Surbiton set up an action group in 1974, to foster the quality of life in the Victorian town. Anxious about derelict shops and the state of the shopping areas, they formed a central area committee.

Posters on the wall advertise concerts by Humble Pie and McGuinness Flint at the Civic Hall, Guildford, the Four Tops and the Delfonics at the Hammersmith Odeon and David Essex "in his own spectacular show" in London.

This shop stood next to Henry Roberts, the outfitters at the bottom end of Victoria Road. Carrying the handbag is Eunice Paxman, who later stood for the St. Mark's ward in a local by-election.

*Paula Yates complained of dirty sheets*

# Boomtown Rats move to Chessington

**Bob Geldof, centre, and the Boomtown Rats, pictured in 1978 during their year-long stay at Chessington. Johnny Fingers, wearing pyjamas, was sometimes seen shopping in Hook, still wearing his night attire. This photograph was taken by former Kingston schoolteacher, Adrian Boot.**

Chessington was the home of the Boomtown Rats, in 1977. Bob Geldof and his fellow musicians were often spotted sauntering around the local shopping parades. On at least one occasion, the group's pianist, Johnny Fingers, was seen going into the Midland Bank at Hook, wearing just his pyjamas. Bob, and girlfriend, Paula Yates, were sometimes spotted in Hook's Nat West Bank.

The new wave band lived and worked at Barwell Court, a spacious farm estate at Leatherhead Road, just a stone's throw from Chessington Zoo.

Formed in Ireland, in 1975, the Boomtown Rats caught the attention of the music press by acting and dressing outrageously at their Irish gigs. As their fame grew, Geldof took the band to London where they were turned down by both the United

Artists and Island record companies, and were only offered a "trifling amount" by Decca, which they refused.

Soon after, Virgin offered them a £1million contract which, surprisingly, they turned down in favour of a less demanding, yet more profitable, deal with Ensign, committing them to just three albums instead of Virgin's 10 LPs in five years.

In August 1977, " Looking After No.1," became the Rats' first chart hit. It was followed by "Mary Of The Fourth Form," in November 1977 and "She's So Modern," "Like Clockwork" and "Rat Trap," the following year.

The historic mansion at Barwell Court, which had once been given by King Henry VIII to one of his mistresses, was ideal for the Rats.

By chance it was owned by Virgin Records and one of the spacious rooms had been soundproofed, making it suitable for rehearsing music in.

Mutt Lange, a top record producer, heard the lads play at their Chessington home, at first saying they were "terrible" but later changing his mind.

After a triumphant year in 1977, the Rats, with two hits under their belts, decided to return to Ireland and later tour the United States and Canada, staying at Chessington in between. Geldof wrote most of the Rats' second album, "Tonic For The Troops," while at Barwell Court. There was plenty of time to concentrate on song-writing because the band had no friends in the London area.

"I would stay in and write songs while the others tossed around," he once wrote.

In his book, *Is That It?,* Bob Geldof writes: "Chessington was like a calm awakening," after their exhaustive touring. Following one tour he rang up Paula Yates, whom he had met on occasions in Dublin and who was then staying in London. "I suggested she come back to Chessington."

He rang her from a London club. "There was a screech of brakes and she was outside, in a taxi, almost as soon as I put the 'phone down.

She had brought with her two huge suitcases, the size lady explorers used to take into African jungles, on the heads of a train of native porters,"Geldof recalls in his autobiography. 'I hope she doesn't think she's been invited permanently,' I thought. When we got back to Chessington, I asked her to stay down-stairs and make some tea while I rushed up to my room and kicked all the dirty underwear, and other unsavouries, under my bed. She was not impressed."

The book states that paula Yates, appalled by the dirty sheets, returned next day with a new set, saying: "I've got rid of the old ones. I hope you don't mind. I got a nice set with little flowers on."

Paula was teased by some of the Rats, at Chessington, about her lack of culinary skills. Allegedly she had never cooked a meal before. She told Fingers, one day, that she would prepare a meal for Bob.

This involved getting the train to London, visiting Harrod's, and returning to Barwell Court with £27-worth of steaks, tomatoes, mushrooms, potatoes and a ready-made dessert.

She queried how people could afford to eat at such prices. Then she burnt the first course "to a cinder." Thereafter the band would gather around on Saturday evenings to study Paula's latest culinary attempts.

After an extensive American tour, the option on Barwell Court ran out and Geldof, then 24, decided to move to a house in Clapham.

Seven years later, he organized the world-famous Band Aid operation to help famine-stricken Ethiopia.

**A poster on a Ewell building in the early part of the Seventies, advertising a gig at Wallington Public Hall, Stafford Road.**

# Opening of Malden Underpass

Malden Underpass, on the A3, was opened on Wednesday 18th August, 1976, after a protest by anti-cars campaigner, Mollie Worthy, aged 51, from St. Leonard's Road, Surbiton. She briefly halted the opening ceremony, standing in the road and urging pedestrians on the bridge above to come down and protest. Police struggled to get Mrs Worthy into a waiting police Rover car, before she was driven to New Malden police station. Later she was released, without charge. Mrs Worthy, who also fought against the Esher bypass, died at Petersfield in Hampshire, in the early 1990s. Her coffin was taken to the funeral in a horse and cart.

The first traffic starts to flow through the Malden Underpass.

Malden residents watch the opening of the new road in August 1976.

# A stormy start to 1976

**Actor John Alderton, 30, the star of television's popular television programme, Please Sir, moved, with his wife, from their Chelsea flat to Woodham, near Byfleet, in 1970.**

## LOCAL TOP 10

1 **I'm Still Waiting—**Diana Ross.
2 **Never Ending Song of Love—**New Seekers.
3 **It's Too Late—**Carole King.
4 **Let Your Yeah Be Yeah—**Pioneers.
5 **Nathan Jones—**Supremes.
6 **What Are You Doing Sunday—**Dawn.

**The top ten records in the last week of August 1971, compiled from sales at Rhythms Record Shop at Station Road, Redhill.**

The new year was only two days old when a violent gale rampaged across Britain during the evening of Friday 2nd January, leaving 26 people dead and a repair bill exceeding £100million. The most tumultuous winds bypassed Surrey and devastated the Midlands and East Anglia but nevertheless, in the Kew, Richmond, and Kingston area, gusts of wind, exceeded hurricane force reaching 80mph.

In the south of Surrey, in the Horley area, 65mph was recorded and it was remarkably mild at the height of the storm, with 56F (13.3C). In Bushy Park, near Hampton Court, many large, splendid trees were felled and some were spread-eagled in all directions.

Tenants from a block of council flats had to evacuate their homes as the gable ends were blown out. Bricks rained down, flattening a Mini-van and a Ford Cortina, while a man driving a BMW had a miraculous escape when a tree standing in the grounds of Normansfield Hospital, Hampton, came hurtling down on to his car as he was driving past, crushing the rear of the vehicle, but he escaped unscathed.

Among the most hazardous incidents of the evening, were the heroic exploits of Hampton waterman, George Kenton, who saw that the powerful gusts of wind were tearing cruisers and dinghies from their moorings along the river.

A sailing boat, parked on the shore, was lifted into the air and flung into the river. Mr. Kenton launched a dinghy and went in hot pursuit. For three gale-lashed hours he struggled to round up the vessels.

The wind was so strong that it whipped up clouds of spray almost as far as Hampton Court Road, but he succeeded in berthing most of the boats.

At Calverleigh Way, Worcester Park, bricks were blown out of the wall of a house, above a bedroom, showering masonry all over the garden. Flying sheets of iron were hurled from a house under repair, plummeting on to adjacent properties. Some sheets were wrapped around trees.

At Esher and Walton, many roads were blocked by falling trees, one narrowly missing a passing bus in Lammas Lane, Walton, whilst a silver birch tree in Pelham's Walk, Esher, squashed a car only half-an-hour after the owner had parked in his driveway.

Trees also blocked 13 roads in Epsom and Ewell but for most people who stayed indoors, to escape the storm, the evening was characterized by flickering lamps and television screens as cables shorted on the national electricity grid.

One abiding memory from Ian Currie, in his Wallington maisonette, was the wail of the wind blowing through the letterbox. Every strong gust would produce a sound akin to a wartime air raid siren. The weather was to hit the headlines again later in the year, fierce winds being exchanged for blazing sunshine.

**Clarence Street, Kingston, with one-way traffic, in 1975. Mac market supermarket is on the left, next to Rowe's fashions, and on the right is C&A.**

## *A year of industrial problems*

# Kingston in 1975

Industrial problems were rife in Kingston as New Year 1975 dawned. Consultants in the town started to work to rule, early in January, in protest over the new terms of contract offered by the Social Services Secretary, Mrs Barbara Castle.

On 15th January, the Secretary of State for Industry, Mr Tony Wedgwood Benn, announced that Hawker Siddeley Aviation, including its Kingston division of over 3,000 workers, was to be merged with Hawker Siddeley Dynamics (guided weapons) and BAC, to form a national British aircraft industry. The unions feared job losses in the future.

Work was due to start on a £400,000 hostel for single, homeless people, at the Kaleidoscope Centre at Bunyan Baptist Church. The complex was to include a chapel, two surgeries, and an underground discotheque club. The Reverend Eric Blakebrough felt the cost of the scheme, and the £175,000 funding from Kingston Council, was justified, when compared with the cost of placing youths in care. Rivermead School's fifth-formers hit out at the raising of the school-leaving age by launching their own magazine to air their views. One student wrote: "Soon I will leave school a year later than before and all that will have happened to me is that I will have lost a year of my careering life."

On Tuesday, 11th February, 1975, a murder took place in Kingston town centre. A man entered Cray's fashion store, in Clarence Street, and stabbed Mrs Helen Hayes in the neck and back. Mrs Hayes, 60, was the manageress. A man was later arrested.

Students planned five days of protests over the Government's cut-backs in education spending. The students claimed that 800 teacher-training places at Gipsy Hill College, Kingston Hill, would be reduced by half as the financial axe fell.

Hundreds of residents from the Canbury Park area attended a protest meeting as a result of

**Members of the union NALGO, near County Hall, Kingston, on 17th February, 1976, in protest at Surrey County Council's proposed £3½ million cuts to services covering libraries, adult education and remedial facilities as well as those for the mentally handicapped. A placard reads: "1½ p on your rates can't mean much to you but it could mean my whole future."**

plans to develop the estate into an industrial park. In early March a bus driver, leaving Kingston Garage, was hit over the head by a youth who was wielding an iron bar. Another youth was sent to Borstal for holding up, at knife-point, the driver of an RF 216 bus, in Wood Street, Kingston.

A plan to reduce traffic in Richmond Park, came under fire in March 1975. The D.o.E. planned a clockwise one-way system around the park, so that cars entering at Ham gate could only reach Kingston by driving via Sheen and Robin Hood Gates.

The mild winter of 1975 was blamed for the downhill trend in sledge sales. Spires, the sports shop in Eden Street, only sold one sledge in a month.

In April of the same year, hundreds of manual workers marched on the Guildhall, Kingston, to protest over the council's handling of a district auditor's report on bonus irregularities and to seek reassurances on security of jobs.

Education Secretary, Reg Prentice, tried to force the hand of Kingston Council to turn all its schools into comprehensives. Kingston Grammar School warned of large fees if it was to go independent.

Coombe Wood Golf Course lost 500 trees to Dutch Elm Disease and was said to be: "A shadow of its former self."

Shoppers complained about getting electric shocks from coathangers in Kingston's C&A store. The staff arranged for the new carpet to be treated with anti-static spray.

A semi-detached house, with four good-sized bedrooms, in Hampton Wick, was advertised for £32,000 in June 1975 and a three-bedroomed, Georgian-style town house, between Kingston Hill and Ham was priced at £23,900.

A £54million scheme to develop the second stage of the Eden Walk shopping and office complex, in Kingston, hit financial setbacks in June.

Showing at Kingston's ABC cinema, in mid-June 1975, were: It's Alive (X) and Band Lands (X), while at the Granada 1, Young Frankenstein (AA) was being screened. Granada 3 was advertising Reluctant Virgin (X) and Red Hot In Bed (X). The nearby Studio 7s programme included Take This To My Body (X) and "16" (X).

Kingston's newest pub, the crown-shaped Seven Saxons, was still standing empty in late June 1975. A builders' strike and shortage of materials were blamed for its delayed opening.

Partial pedestrianisation of Kingston Market

**The entrance to Brady's Arcade, Kingston, c.1973. This remarkable collection of stores, selling bric-a-brac, was a favourite feature of Eden Street, and when it closed it was much-mourned by shoppers and browsers.**

Place was to be tried out after the GLC agreed plans on a trial basis.

In early July 1975, the Government announced a deferral of plans to nationalize Hawker, the aircraft manufacturers. The town's MP, Mr Norman Lamont, said he was delighted.

At the end of July, refectory staff at Kingston College of Further Education demonstrated outside the building, in protest against Kingston Council's decision to bring in outside caterers.

The showing of uncensored sex films at Studio Seven in Kingston, was attacked by Baptist minister, Reverend Blakebrough. He told the *Kingston Borough News*: "I might have more sympathy for a prostitute than for the people responsible for this exploitation."

Plans were drawn up for a new £1.2million shopping complex at The Tannery site in Thames Street, Kingston.

The very hot summer weather was blamed for the death of 100 ducks on the Thames, between Kingston and Hampton Court. A toxic algae, which formed on reeds in heatwaves, was thought to have been the cause.

The Hawker aircraft company received another boost when it became heavily involved with the development of a "Harrier Carrier" aircraft.

A warning from health officials went out to people who had bought parrots from Pets Cavalcade, in Richmond Road, Kingston, where a parrot disease had been discovered.

It was all-change on the buses serving route 65 (Ealing - Richmond - Kingston - Chessington Zoo), when the fleet of RT models was changed to the RM Routemasters, by London Transport, on 5th October 1975. The RTs had served the area since the 1940s.

The larger Routemasters could carry an extra eight passengers per vehicle. From 3rd November, the route was extended during school hours, to the Fox and Hounds, Malden Rushett.

Huge financial cutbacks and a reduction in manpower, continued to cause problems in the borough council's work during October, but the go-ahead was given for the £5.4million Eden Walk shopping centre scheme, despite fears.

Approval was also given by the council for a shops and offices development behind the Knapp Drewett printing works, in Church Street. By mid-October, Kingston Grammar School announced it was going completely independent in 1976, with fees of up to £750 per annum.

Boat owners at Buckland's Wharf, Kingston, were ordered by the council to remove their vessels by 6th December, sparking a massive controversy. They were later given a six-months' stay of execution.

In November, a work-to-rule by junior doctors at Kingston Hospital resulted in emergency cases, only, being admitted.

*A browser's paradise and a famous dummy*

# Brady's Arcade and 'Old Lil'

**Reg Siddons, one of Kingston's best-known traders in the Seventies, stands forlornly in the derelict Brady's Arcade c.1974, shortly before the site was cleared for redevelopment in Eden Street. He had formerly kept five stores in the bric-a-brac browsers' paradise parade.**

One of Kingston's most irrepressible traders was Reg Siddons, who kept five stores in Brady's Arcade, off Eden Street, until its demolition was proposed in 1973. Brady's Arcade was a collector's paradise of Aladdin's cave-like shops, all under one roof. Curious shoppers would browse for hours, through the irregular piles of bric-a-brac, as they looked for bargains.

Even more famous than Reg Siddons, was Old Lil, a dishevelled female dummy, which stood outside Brady's Arcade, attired in a motley assortment of period clothes.

At one end of the arcade was a large hole in a wall, through which shoppers passed to make their way to Clarence Street, by way of Pratt's Passage. When there was a proposal by Kingston Corporation to seal up the illegal hole, angry traders took action and launched a petition. So fierce was the opposition to the plan that, when workmen arrived with bricks, sand and cement, the labourers were forced to abandon their goods and flee the scene.

Some 2,500 shoppers signed a petition calling for the council to abandon its plan to re-brick the hole. Traders, who included Gerry Altman, elec-

trician, and Johnny Martin, hairdresser, claimed that up to 10,000 people passed through the arcade on a Saturday and they would be greatly inconvenienced, and endangered, if they had to use the nearby roads instead. The campaigners were granted a short reprieve .

When Brady's Arcade was pulled down, many tears were shed. The council offered the shopkeepers a new site, by the river, calling it the Clattern Antiques Centre, but few people were prepared to make a long detour to visit it.

Two years later Reg decided to take over two shop units next to Kingston Station. One he used for bric-a-brac and the other for newspapers, paperback books and records.

Reg, who was helped by his son, Barrie, had previously worked on "every market in London." Once he acquired thousands of false teeth, forceps and drills, from a retired dental surgeon. He sold the lot to a man who drilled the teeth to make necklaces. Reg's stock phrase was "Anything is saleable." On one early occasion he got his hands on a photograph which had once belonged to Al Capone and a cigarette card collection which had belonged to King Farouk.

**Reg Siddons, with the famous dummy, Old Lil, which stood outside his bric-a-brac stores in the Seventies. Reg moved to this Curiosity Shop, next to Kingston Station, in 1973, after leaving Brady's Arcade, which had been compulsorily purchased for town centre redevelopment.**

**A busy day at the market place, in Kingston town centre, in 1975. Harrow Passage, leading to the Apple Market, runs alongside Guvnors fashion shop.**

Some of the young walkers, from Kingston, who went on a riverside ramble in aid of charity, early in October 1975. From left to right are: Tina Memory, Carol Ray, Dawn Archer, Karen Johnson, Adrian Hall, Mark Sheehan.

A flower seller tends to customers' needs in the ancient market place, Kingston, in 1975.

Hawker Siddeley Aviation's premises, Richmond Road, Kingston, in 1975, when it was one of the borough's biggest employers. It was demolished in the Eighties.

Cars, buses and lorries trundle along Clarence Street, Kingston, c.1975, many years before pedestrianisation resulted in cars only being allowed to turn left into Eden Street. On Saturdays, shoppers were still squeezed onto narrow pavements, risking injury if they stepped off the kerb.

The cattle market end of Fairfield, Kingston, in 1975. The museum is on the left and work is under way on a high-rise office block on the right. Parked outside the Wimpey site is a Fyffes banana lorry.

Jimmy Tarbuck, Peter Goodright and Roy Castle promise lots of laughs at the Regal Social Club, Richmond Road, Kingston, in September 1974.

A 215 single-decker bus, to Church Cobham, joins the flow of traffic streaming past, and behind, Kingston Station. Twenty years after this picture had been taken, in 1975, cars and lorries travelled in the other direction, after major changes to the town's one-way system.

Left: headlines from the *Daily Mail*, dated 11th November 1976, in which there is a report about the terrible murder at Ham Parade. Right: the *Daily Express*, by that date a tabloid, reveals, on 3rd November, 1977, how the killer had been out on bail when he murdered Angela Woolliscroft.

## *Snatched £2,500 then fired fatal shots*

# Gunman shoots bank girl dead

The population of Kingston and Richmond was left stunned, in November 1976, when a gunman shot a clerk dead at Barclays Bank in Ham Parade. Twenty-one-year-old Angela Woolliscroft, of Newlands Way, Hook, was the first bank employee, anywhere in the U.K., to be killed on duty, by raiders, since a murder at Worthing, in 1961. Following the latter-mentioned incident, the culprit was later hanged.

Angela, a hockey enthusiast, handed over £2,500 to 39-year-old Michael George Hart, from the Basingstoke area. He was currently out on bail for other serious offences and was wanted by Paris police in connection with the stabbing of a cabby. He grabbed the cash from Angela and then shot her dead.

The news was splashed all over the daily papers' front pages the next day, 11th November.

After his conviction, Hart told police he had disposed of the gun in the River Thames. He burned all other evidence, including his raincoat, wig and gloves and hid the money, from the raid, in his garage.

On 3rd November, 1977, at the Old Bailey, Hart was jailed for life, with the judge's recommendation that he be detained for at least 25 years. Hart was also sentenced to further jail terms totalling 92 years, to run concurrently with the life sentence, on 21 other offences, a further 42 offences being considered.

The *Kingston Borough News* tells of the tragedy and reports how Angela Woolliscroft was a former member of Claygate Hockey Club.

Two weeks after Angela Woolliscroft's murder, a Kingston schoolboy, Vincent Livermore, was found dead on a bomb site at Church Road, Kingston. The 13-year-old pupil of Rivermead School had been battered around the head with a blunt instrument. A 15-year-old Kingston boy was later charged.

Comedian and singer, Harry Secombe, who lived in Sutton, paid a visit to Bentalls department store in Kingston, early in November 1975, to sign copies of his book, Goon For Lunch. The star also called at the now-vanished Royal Charter public house, in nearby Richmond Road, where he launched a charity competition. This pub, formerly the Three Fishes, until its name change in 1971, was to close in 1986. A relief road later ran through the site of the pub.

Eden Street, Kingston, in 1975. On the right is the Freeman Hardy Willis shoe shop, and Percy Harrison, high class menswear.

Harry Secombe relaxes at the Royal Charter pub, Kingston, during his visit to the town, in November 1975.

**Bentalls' Corner, Kingston, in 1975. Lower Ham Road and Wood Street are to the right of the Bentalls' car park. Bentalls' restaurant is on the right, in the foreground.**

NORMAN Lamont, Conservative, became MP for Kingston on Thames, in May 1972. He won with a 10,307 majority, leaving S.T.E. Wells, Liberal, in second place and Labour hopeful, C.J.Mullins, in third.

Mr Lamont held the position until October 1995 when the majority of the constituency was merged with Surbiton and the remainder with Richmond. He lost his seat to the sitting Surbiton Tory, Richard Tracey.

Born in Lerwick, Shetland, in 1942, Mr Lamont was educated at Cambridge where he joined the Conservative Association in 1963 and became president of the Cambridge Union in 1964. In 1965, he became personal assistant to Rt. Hon. Duncan Sandys, MP. After working in the Conservative Research department, between 1966 and 1968, he became a merchant banker with Rothschild and Sons from 1968 to 1979. He was appointed Opposition Spokesman on prices and consumer affairs (1975-76); industry (1976-79) and was Parliamentary Under Secretary of State in the energy department between 1979 and 1981.

**Norman Lamont, Kingston's MP, in an early Seventies family picture, with his wife, Rosemary, whom he married in 1971. The couple have two children.**

The Seven Saxons was one of the shortest-lived public houses in Kingston's history. It opened in Eden Street, right in the middle of the town centre, in November 1975. Civic dignitaries attended the opening ceremony and shire horses pulled up outside the seven-sided Courage building to publicize the new, arty inn. Sadly, by November 1983, its closure was imminent. The Seven Saxons had attracted the noisier element of Kingston's locals, during its existence. The building remained and in latter years was used as a building society. In January, 1975, another Eden Street pub closed down. This was the Three Compasses, which was later pulled down to make way for part of the Eden Walk shopping centre. In April 1975, expansion plans by Kingston College of Further Education, resulted in the demolition, later on, of the Gloucester Arms. This pub, in The Bittoms, was once the haunt of top racing driver, Jack Brabham, who owned a garage at Hook.

Preparations for Kingston Carnival, 1976, involved publicizing the event on this L-reg. van. Here the van has pulled up in Hook Road, Hook, opposite homes in Green end. Organized by the Lions, the event included a wrestling match between Bobby Barnes and Vic Faulkner, at Surbiton Assembly Rooms, plus a carnival tattoo at RAF Chessington, near Hook.

A notable feature of Kingston's skyline was the two power station chimneys which towered 250 feet above the ground.  Built in 1948, the reinforced concrete structures became redundant in 1980 when the power station closed, for good, on 31st  October.  This is a 1975 picture of the chimneys in Lower Ham Road.  Also standing proud is the tower of All Saints' Church, rebuilt in this style after a previous steeple was demolished in the great hurricane of November, 1703, and which was chronicled by Daniel Defoe, the author of *Robinson Crusoe*.

Cars queuing for a dwindling supply of petrol in December 1973. A four-gallons-only restriction was on the cards in December 1973, owing to the national shortage. On 26th November, Peter Walker, the Secretary for Trade and Industry, told the House of Commons that the Government was printing 16 million petrol ration books. On 5th December, a 50mph compulsory limit was introduced to save fuel. This picture shows motorists waiting hopefully at the Willment Garage in Twickenham.

## *Petrol shortage and a 50mph limit*

# Richmond and Twickenham

The fleet of vehicles used by Richmond Council's Social Services in May 1975. By now the fuel crisis had passed.

Twickenham on a busy day in December 1977. An RM 281 bus negotiates the traffic on the other side of the road.

Roger Dean, the rock album artist, so well-known in the Seventies for his record covers, opened But Is It Art, a shop at Golden Court, Richmond, run by Malcolm Walker of Ham. The contemporary rock group, Yes, made much use of Roger's talents.

BRITAIN'S BIGGEST EVENING SALE

# Evening News

LONDON: FRIDAY SEPTEMBER 16 1977 8p

CITY PRICES

## Pop star killed when car hits tree at 5 a.m.

# MARC BOLAN DIES IN CRASH

MARC BOLAN and American singer Gloria Jones. She was driving the car and suffered a broken jaw.

**Evening News Reporters**

POP star Marc Bolan, 29, was killed instantly in a car crash in Barnes early today.

He was a passenger in a purple Mini which hit a tree in Queens Ride, near the junction with Gipsy Lane, just after 5 a.m.

The driver was Bolan's common-law wife black American singer Gloria Jones, 30. She broke her jaw and was taken to Queen Mary's Hospital, Roehampton.

The 1275 Mini GT, registration number FOX 661 L, was a write-off. The front windows and windscreen were shattered and parts of the engine pushed into the passenger seat.

Mr. Richard Jones, Gloria's brother,

was travelling in a car behind them.

He told police that the Mini was doing about 30 mph just before the crash.

It is thought they were all going to Bolan's home in Richmond Road West, Sheen, about two miles away.

The crash scene is a notorious accident black spot.

Miss Jones's car had just crossed a hump-backed bridge over a railway line when it ploughed through a thin wire fence and crashed into a horse chestnut tree.

The impact crushed the front and spun it round in the road.

Mr. Philip Evans-Lowe, who was travelling to work at a local dairy, said: "When I arrived a girl was lying on the bonnet and a man with long dark curly hair was stretched out in the road.

"There was a hell of a mess. I rushed to get the police."

### 'Cover him'

Lying in the mini was a badge with the inscription: "Every day is a holy day."

A jumper, the latest edition of the New Musical Express and a book about Eric Clapton were strewn about the back seat.

Mrs. Ziki Robinson, who lives nearby said: "There was an almighty bang.

"The man in the second car was a

year ended up by their boundary wall.

She said today: "It is definitely a very angerous spot. Although the area is not in m husband's ward, he is very concerned about it."

Bolan's press agent Keith Altham said when told of the crash: "Oh my God. This has come as a terrible shock. I have been a friend of his for about 1¼ years."

Mr. Altham did not know why Bolan would have been driving through Barnes early today, but he understood that he had been seeing his manager, Mr. Tony Howard, until late last night.

Bolan has just finished recording a six-week TV series titled Marc which is nationally televised each Wednesday at 4.15 p.m.

### 'Very concerned'

The final show with his long-time friend David Bowie as guest star is scheduled for September 28.

His latest single Celebrate Summer has so far failed to hit the top fifty.

T-Rex were the top group in the country in 1971, selling more than 6,000,000 records.

Bolan's real name was Marc Feld. His wife of four years, artist June Feld divorced him last October because of his adultery with Gloria Jones, 30, an

People were shocked when news broke that pop star, Marc Bolan, of the group T-Rex, had died in a car crash on 16th September, 1977. He was 29. The accident occurred at Queen's Ride, Barnes Common, near Richmond, when a purple Mini, driven by his girlfriend, the singer Gloria Jones, collided with a tree, at 5am. Bolan, who lived at Richmond Road West, Sheen, was, in the Sixties, a member of the band John's Children, from Leatherhead and Fetcham. For music fans there was a double blow. A month earlier, to the day, Elvis Presley was found dead at his home, Graceland, in Memphis. He was 42.

Richmond and Twickenham schoolchildren in December 1972, the month Chuck Berry's controversial hit, "My Ding-A-Ling" was at number one and the Osmonds' "Crazy Horses" was lodged at number two in the charts.

A suggestion on a wall in Grosvenor Road, Twickenham, where, in May 1973, allegations concerning the lifestyles of young people living there was described as "total lies" by the young inhabitants. They had been accused of excessive noise, naked appearances in garden parties and of breaking windows.

Film stars Madeline Smith (above), Hywel Bennett and other stars of the screen, came to Richmond on Sunday, 30th December 1973, to launch the opening of Richmond Odeon's new triple cinema.

A member of Teddington youth club exhibits an entry in its fashion show held on Tuesday, 1st May, 1973. Special guest at the event was Patrick Cargill from TV's "Father, dear father."

Three men, with ammonia sprays, raided the sub post office in Friars Stile Road, Richmond, on Wednesday, 10th October, 1973. In a car chase which ensued, a police Rover 3500 overturned in Kew Road, Richmond. George and Doris Littlejohn, of the Hill Top newsagents and post office, were temporarily blinded in the robbery.

A woman and four children escaped unhurt when this blue Triumph and a lorry collided in The Quadrant, Richmond, in June 1973. Casualty, Mrs Frances Baker, of Ashburton Road, Ham, was badly shaken.

Cliff Richard called into the offices of World Records, at Parkshot, Richmond, on Thursday 1st May, 1975, to collect a silver disc for sales of his six-record set, The Cliff Richard Story. The record later earned him a gold disc.

Take your own rubbish to the tip - these young women became DIY dustmen during the strike by refuse collectors in the Richmond borough during April 1977. Piles of rubbish mounted in the streets, leading to fears of rats and flies.

Children wave their Union Jack flags at Richmond Bridge, in 1977, to celebrate the Queen's Silver Jubilee.

They come in twos. A reporter from the *Richmond and Twickenham Times* waited 45 minutes for a 71 bus in November 1976 - and then a pair arrived together. The service was described by a Ham man as "The Loch Ness Monster." You occasionally spotted it.

January sales at Owen and Owen, in 1978.

Bold autumn colours and designs in fine wool, set the style at a fashion show on 3rd October, 1973, in Sirron House, Vine Road, Barnes. The event was organized by Dickens and Jones, of George Street, Richmond, to raise money for the Richmond and Twickenham branch of the Save the Children fund.

April showers were of snow in 1978. On 11th April, people in Richmond, and elsewhere in Surrey, woke up to a winter wonderland. Here, children make a snowman in Richmond Park, after a heavy overnight fall.

A train drivers' work-to-rule disrupted Southern Region trains all over Surrey and South London in November 1973. Here, Richmond commuters attempt to work out routes to their destinations. Those people who chose to drive, instead, found a gloomy situation on the roads. Side streets were only half lit because of an imposed 50 per cent cut in street lighting, to save fuel.

**Plenty of enticements to fill up with fuel at this petrol station in Rose Hill, including the offer of treble Green Shield stamps. The picture was taken in 1970, before decimalisation.**

## *Wallington, Worcester Park, Carshalton and Belmont*

# Sutton and Cheam in 1973

The beginning of January saw the borough still reeling from the shock of the smash hit by-election victory for the Liberals.

Graham Tope was voted in, turning a Tory majority of around 12,000 at the previous election, into a 7,000 Liberal advantage, the biggest swing in modern times, with Labour losing their deposit. The election had been caused by the resignation of Sir Richard Sharples, in order that he could take up his new commission as Governor of Bermuda.

Mr Tope was soon in action, coming to the aid of four elderly unmarried ladies who were being harassed by an unscrupulous landlord into leaving their rented houses. Walls had been pulled down, rooms were littered with building rubble and cement was poured into their drains. The eventual successful battle to prosecute the landlord and impose more than just a nominal fine was to take the entire year.

In early January, figures were published which revealed that 12 per cent of Sutton's schoolchildren went on from sixth form to university, some four per cent above the national average. However, the "great education debate" as to whether Sutton should have a three-tier pattern of comprehensive education was to rumble on throughout the year and a petition comprising 86,000 signatures, organized by parents opposed to the idea, was sent to the Education Minister — a certain Margaret Thatcher.

Notices appeared in public places announcing that Dorchester Road School, Worcester Park, at the time supplying education for five-to-seven-year-olds, would have a school roll of 400 children aged five-to-nine. However, the school did not exist and was merely an allotment site, which prompted one parent to question whether his son would receive an education if he sent him to the vegetable plots.

There was concern over the demise of the traditional Sunday joint. Beef prices had more than doubled over three years. At Hearns in Wrythe Lane, Carshalton, beef was selling at 54p a pound whilst very little meat was being sold at Newton Centre, Wallington. Grocery bills, too, had soared

**Traffic was re-routed during the summer of 1978, with Sutton High Street in the first stage of banishing motor vehicles and becoming a pedestrian precinct.**

15 per cent in a six-month period, according to the Sutton and District Consumer Group. Eggs were now 19p a half-dozen, bacon was 64p per pound and margarine cost 5½ p.

On Thursday 1st February, during the morning rush hour, a crane jib swung out on to the junction of Cheam and St. James Road and ripped into the top deck of a passing bus. Passengers ducked when they saw the jib pitch towards the vehicle and moments later the impact showered them all with glass as the roof of the bus was torn upwards. Twelve people were treated for cuts and bruises, but it could have been much worse. Later that year, the foreman at the building site was prosecuted for failing to properly supervise operations that morning.

The continuing increase in traffic on the borough's roads was highlighted by a distressing incident, which led to the death of old-age pensioner, Mrs Agnes Mcguire. She had waited nearly an hour to cross the busy Brighton Road in Sutton. The incessant roar of the traffic forced her to stay on the kerb. Motorists were unaware of her plight until she could stand waiting no longer and took a few faltering steps, straight into the path of an oncoming car and was fatally injured.

In May alone, nine people were killed on Surrey's roads. The position was not eased by the 5,000-plus people waiting to take their driving tests. A new Ford Cortina 1600L four-door was advertised at a price of £993 plus VAT or a Vauxhall Viva for £803, although because of labour disputes, there was an acute shortage of new models from several manufacturers.

June did bring some fine, dry conditions. No rain fell during the first fortnight and on 16th June, with the mercury at 77F (25C), the BBC weatherman, Graham Parker, in appropriately glorious sunshine. opened Sutton Hospital's summer fête. He lived in Banstead.

The drought, exacerbated by the previous dry winter, led to a warning by the Sutton and District Water Company that restrictions on the use of water might have to be imposed, because consumption was rising by six million gallons per day. The water company drilled to record depths beneath the chalk, some 370 feet, to tap sufficient water.

Residents at Quarry Park Road, Cheam, were among those who had received leaflets from the water company, asking them to reduce water consumption. Their houses were adjacent to a sports

The busy A232 through Carshalton is particularly narrow adjacent to the pond and great care is needed in negotiating oncoming traffic. There had been twelve crashes in the eight months prior to May 1978, when a car driven by an elderly couple from Ashford plummeted into the water. Fortunately they were not injured, but the operation to retrieve the car, with the aid of a crane, took three hours.

**Early morning and a quieter moment in Sutton High Street in June 1978. Soon afterwards a new traffic scheme was introduced, making the High Street a pedestrianized area**

ground and they became somewhat puzzled as to why a sprinkler had been in constant use on the pitches — the owners of the ground were the Sutton Water Board!

The national "Plant a Tree in '73" campaign was well-received by local schools with, for example, Devonshire Primary School planting a rowan, but the council, when asked how many they had planted, revealed that the total was — none. The reason was that the staff had been engaged in cutting down many trees suffering with Dutch Elm Disease. June also brought the dreaded parking meters to Sutton and had the effect of clearing the streets of parked vehicles. Wardens had very little to do, with few motorists prepared to pay 5p, or a "shilling" as it was still called.

Three schoolboys made the headlines, but all for very different reasons. Cliff James, 18, was appointed onto the board of governors at Glastonbury High School, nominated by Young Socialists. He was one of the first in the country to take up such a post. It caused a storm of protest among Conservative members of the board, which also served in running Sutton Common High School for Girls.

Cliff became an overnight star after appearing on Thames Television, who also wished to film his

first board meeting. However, this request was turned down by the Sutton schools sub-committee. Perhaps not surprisingly, the headmaster and headmistress of the two schools failed to attend the meeting. As for Cliff, he was described as being "quietly helpful."

Schoolboy David Walters died at Sutton West High School after being stabbed by fellow pupil, Kwai Ping Chueng. Kwing Ping was cleared of murder and manslaughter at the Old Bailey after it had been found that he had been bullied and victimized by the deceased and only took the knife to school in order to scare his tormentor.

A Sutton lady celebrated her 112th birthday. Mrs Alice Stevenson received a telegram from Sutton's MP, Graham Tope, which read: "Congratulations to my oldest constituent, top of the poll in Sutton and Cheam." Mrs Stevenson was born on 10th July 1861, when Palmerston was in office in Great Britain and Abraham Lincoln was President of the United States. She credited the avoidance of television as a contributory factor in her longevity. Six weeks later she passed away at Brambleacres old people's home, Worcester Road, Sutton.

The year 1973 was a troubled one as far as industrial relations were concerned. A SEGAS

All over Sutton, street parties were organized, to celebrate the Queen's silver jubilee in early June 1977. The children of Barrington Road are seen here on 9th June, tucking into the ice cream. It was a very chilly day, so thick jumpers were needed to keep warm.

**A scene at the end of the decade, looking north towards the traffic lights at Stafford Road and Woodcote Road, Wallington. The United Reformed Church at the crossroads was a well-known landmark but it has now been demolished.**

strike led to issue of leaflets, delivered with the morning milk, warning customers to keep a constant eye on gas jets, to turn off appliances at night and not to go out of the house while food was still cooking in the oven. The leaflet was directed at customers who were on town gas and in Wallington alone, there were still 20,000 homes so connected and pressure was being reduced. Workers at Mullard's new factory in New Road, Hackbridge, were laid off, following a complete cessation of gas supply.

A "dirty jobs" dispute in March led to patients awaiting treatment in hospitals, such as St.Helier, being told to bring their own bed linen, as 400 workers at the Central Laundry depot, in Muschamp Road, Carshalton, went on a go-slow. In a normal week the depot handled 280,000 pieces of linen. It was not better for those people who were healthy, as rail commuters were affected by an ASLEF go-slow. It was no April Fool either, when VAT was introduced at 10 per cent. A hot-line was introduced to register complaints and queries and it was not long before 400 had

been logged, most to protest against illegal price rises, with launderettes, restaurants and works canteens being the biggest offenders.

A murder caused shock and sadness. The loss was that of Sutton and Cheam's former MP, Sir Richard Sharples, who was brutally assassinated in Bermuda, where he was Governor. Messages of sympathy came from all quarters, including one from the Queen, and the feeling was in complete contrast with the scenes of joy and happiness which had greeted Sir Richard as he drove in an open carriage through the holiday island's streets the previous October, during his inauguration.

Strikes continued to be rife, with a power workers' dispute leading to every alternate street light being turned off in a response by the D.O.E.

The borough was also hit by a petrol famine triggered by the Arab-Israeli conflict in the Middle East. Many garages imposed a limit of three-to-four gallons per customer, though doctors, midwives and other essential users were exempt from restrictions. There was a spate of petrol thefts, the fuel being syphoned from cars.

## SUTTON & CHEAM HERALD

Price 4p  No. 4773  THURSDAY, JULY 5, 1973  *Largest local circulation*

ROYAL VISIT
Pictures —
page 8

### Royal opening of hospital wing named after Bud Flanagan

## QUEEN MOTHER'S VISIT

### Big day at Royal Marsden

THE Queen Mother's visit to Sutton's Royal Marsden Hospital on Tuesday was all too much for pretty 12-years-old Anne Coker.

For Anne, a former patient at the hospital who seven years ago was given only a few months to live, dissolved into tears as she gave Her Majesty a bouquet to mark the opening of the new Bud Flanagan ward.

But the Queen Mother was mobbed. Crowds of cheering sightseers stood in blazing sunshine to catch a glimpse of the Queen Mother as her maroon Rolls-Royce glided smoothly into the hospital grounds.

Hospital staff, who had been preparing for the Royal occasion since 7 am that day, stood by with a discreetly-positioned squad of 20 local police.

Looking cool in her favourite style of dress and coat — floral lilac and white violet with a close-fitting lilac petal hat and white accessories — the Queen Mother stepped gaily along the red carpet.

She was greeted by Lord Lieutenant of Surrey, Lord ... Hamilton, Graham Tope MP, Sutton's mayor Coun Dennis Salari and other civic dignitaries. Inside the foyer, she chatted gaily with hospital administrators, governors, and long serving staff.

Taking time off from the official schedule, she stopped and chatted to staff and patients in the new £800,000 96-bed extension, of which the Bud Flanagan ward is a part.

Clasping the Queen Mother's hand, a woman patient on the verge of tears, blurted out: "You are so beautiful, your Majesty. I never thought I would get to see you."

Moving into the Bud Flanagan isolation ward, the Royal party was greeted by the Crazy Gang comedian's widow, "Curly" Flanagan, actor Derek Nimmo, Bud's friend Chesney Allen, and many others who had given proceeds of their shows to the Bud Flanagan Leukaemia Fund, which ...

MINISTER Mr Edward ... was among leading ...

Died ...

**Headlines from the *Sutton and Cheam Herald* of July 5th 1973.**

Bicycles also went missing. One lorry was drained of 20 gallons, but things were booming for the cycle shops. Two wheels were replacing four as petrol dried up, with ladies' machines doing the best trade, but one could always unwind by going to the cinema and seeing the current blockbuster, The Poseidon Adventure, starring Gene Hackman, Shelley Winters and Red Buttons.

For patients and staff at Sutton's Royal Marsden Hospital, there was no doubt about what was the highlight of their year — a Royal visit. On a fine July day, a maroon Rolls Royce arrived at the hospital and out stepped a vibrant Queen Mother, to open the new Bud Flanagan Ward. The Crazy Gang comedian's only son had died of leukaemia and his wife, "Curly" Flanagan, actor Derek Nimmo and the other half of Flanagan and Allen, Chesney Allen, had helped to raise, along with many other actors and performers, a large part of the £800,000 for the new wing.

The Royal guest took time out to visit many wards, making patients and staff overjoyed. One patient rushed over, bowed and said: "You are very beautiful, so very beautiful. I never thought I would ever meet you."

**The Queen Mother visiting Sutton's Royal Marsden Hospital on 3rd July 1973.**

**At the height of a violent storm during the evening of 11th January 1978 the Windsor Castle public house in Carshalton caught fire and flames, fanned by the gale force winds, gutted the top floor and destroyed the roof, whilst water and smoke badly damaged the bar below.**

## Carshalton pub on fire; winds fan the flames

# Ablaze in a tempest

A tap on the barometer during the day of 11th January 1978 showed the pressure as very low, but during the late afternoon it suddenly rose and that is a recipe for very stormy times ahead. The wind grew in strength and soon, storm force winds were screaming across Surrey.

On the higher parts of the downs, snow fell during the day, giving several inches at Caterham and with torrential rain elsewhere, driving was a nightmare. Teacher, Ian Currie, could hardly open the door of his Ford Corsair as he left de Stafford School, Caterham, while the wind shrieked and tore around the building. It was at about this time that the wind gusted to 80mph at Kew and fire broke out at the Windsor Castle public house at Carshalton.

At around 6.30 pm a passer-by rushed into the pub and said: "You are on fire." The manager and seven customers were oblivious to a blaze which had apparently started in a neon strip light hanging beneath outside guttering. The fierce wind fanned the flames and within seconds an inferno had taken hold. Luckily, everyone managed to escape, including the landlord's family.

The fire brigade strike at the time brought naval fire fighters, utilising their Green Goddess tenders from Croydon. An eyewitness living in nearby cottages said: "As their hoses went up, the wind was blowing the water away." Chunks of material were blown onto neighbouring houses

**Volkswagen's new "big look" Beetle, the 1303, was unveiled in 1972. It featured a re-designed front end, with a deep, curved windscreen for "added safety, improved visibility and increased space." It came with a choice of 1300 cc engine in the standard model or as the 1303S, which had a 1600cc engine. This photograph was sent out to Surrey's newspapers and other publications by the public relations department of VW, at Brighton Road, Purley.**

but the rain probably saved them from catching fire.

Elsewhere, the winds tore down many trees in Bushy Park and a 200-year-old Cedar of Lebanon, a local landmark standing 70 feet in height on the banks of the Thames at Teddington was sent crashing to the ground. Hundreds of trees were felled in the Leith Hill area near Dorking, the conifers all lying poleaxed in a south-easterly direction. An expectant mother was seriously hurt when a tree crashed down onto her Mini as she was driving at Redstone Hill, Redhill. The next morning the amount of gale damage became apparent and Ian Currie wrote in his diary: "Twigs, branches, fences, all blown together in a tangle of confusion. At de Stafford School, Caterham, there was much devastation, with many trees blown down, fences smashed, the bicycle sheds blown away and Burntwood Lane a

melée of branches and splintered trunks. Everything was covered in crusted snow and frozen rain, even making walking a dangerous task."

The fierce north winds, which led to the collapse of several piers, including those at Margate and Skegness, caused a surge in the North Sea and forced tides to within a foot or so of overtopping the Thames embankments. The GLC, the capital-wide authority, urged people to listen out for radio, TV and loudspeaker flood warnings. The London Flood Control Centre, set up to deal with such an emergency, went onto red alert. Ironically, a few weeks later, work started on the Thames flood barrier, a scheme designed to cope with just such an emergency.

As the flames were quelled a forlorn landlord, Mr Alex Requena, said: "It is all burnt out and all I have left are the clothes I am wearing."

Nork Way, Nork, Banstead, c.1971. The Surrey Library newsagents, Cato's hardware and the Nork Pharmacy, are on the left.

## *Candles and Tilley lamps*

# Life in Banstead, 1972

The onset of 1972 was a difficult time for new home buyers, with a 20 per cent increase in house prices during 1971. A terraced house fetched £6,000 and a semi-detached, in a 'pleasant' neighbourhood cost £10,000.

However, a teacher's salary amounted to the princely sum of £60 per month and there was more for them to do this year as the school leaving age went up from 15 to 16 years. According to a local building society, mortgages averaged £5,750, and couples were forced to look as far away as Farnborough, in Hampshire, to find cheaper house prices.

On a snow-covered pile of building rubble at Tangier Wood, Burgh Heath, builders had more to read than just the daily newspaper, in their tea-break. Emerging out of the bricks and mortar came secret police files — hundreds of sheets of paper referring to convictions and enquiries from Putney Police Station.

Renovations at the police station resulted in demolition material being taken to Burgh Heath, to be used as hard core in the construction of a small housing estate, but why confidential documents should be included remained a mystery.

A burst of easterly winds, at the end of January, led briefly to a severe cold spell. The mercury dropped to 9F (-13C) in the Chipstead Valley and several inches of snow carpeted the ground. Two schools, in Merland Rise, Tadworth, had to close because the anthracite fuel, needed for their boilers, ran out.

Interruptions to power supplies, caused by strikes in the power industry, caused chaos. Traffic lights failed, street lamps blacked out and high streets twinkled with flickering candles in shop windows. Surrey stores hired guards to deter shoplifters. The staff at many firms worked on, without heating, but the weather then warmed up a little.

One theatre group, the Chipstead Players, performed "The Chalk Garden" at the Peter Aubertin Hall, illuminated by Tilley lamps, camping lights and spotlights powered by car batteries, and the show went on. At a Banstead launderette, customers had to wait three hours for the washing cycle to complete whilst some patrons lost their patience, opened the machines — and promptly flooded the premises.

Feelings ran high in Lower Kingswood and an

The Star Inn, Hooley, in 1977, just before its closure. Once a farmhouse, it was pulled down to enable the A23 to be straightened. It was a focal point of village life for centuries. Hooley was left without a public house but its name is remembered in Star Lane, which leads up to Chipstead. Many other houses in both Chipstead and Hooley, would have been demolished if plans to expand the M23 from Merstham to Croydon went ahead, but the government abandoned the scheme when it ran out of cash. The road would have bisected the picturesque Chipstead Valley, blighting homes and schools.

action committee was formed when plans were announced to dual part of the carriageway of the A217. Residents were concerned about crossing the road, which would become a busy link to the new M25 intersection on Reigate Hill, at that time due to be completed by 1974. Some 45,000 vehicles a day were then predicted to pass through the village.

The Banstead-Woodmansterne area drew national attention when a nine-year-old girl was assaulted and stabbed in Woodmansterne Woods, at around 5pm on 22nd April.

She was playing hide and seek with friends when a man lured her farther into the woods, with the pretence of finding a ring. He then told her to take her clothes off and then stabbed her. She escaped death by inches and some 40 detectives were assigned to the case in a massive police hunt which included an appeal on the television programme Police Five.

Banstead youngsters were jumping for joy in the summer of 1972, when Banstead Urban District Council, soon to be merged with Reigate, organized play schemes in the summer holidays.

**Epsom racegoers attend The Oaks event, on Saturday 10th June, 1972.**

**The Icelandic fish and chip shop, on the corner of Hook Road and Adelphi Road, Epsom, in 1971. The "chippie" was established in the 1930s, by Alfred Charles Marshall, and his family. He became Epsom and Ewell's mayor in 1942. On the right of the *Evening Standard*'s Mini-van is The Rifleman public house.**

## DERBY WINNERS

| YEAR | WINNER | JOCKEY | BETTING |
|------|--------|--------|---------|
| 1970 | Nijinski | L.Piggott | 11-8F |
| 1971 | Mill Reef | G.Lewis | 110-30F |
| 1972 | Roberto | L.Piggott | 3-1F |
| 1973 | Morston | E.Hide | 25-1 |
| 1974 | Snow Knight | B.Taylor | 50-1 |
| 1975 | Grundy | P.Eddery | 5-1 |
| 1976 | Empery | L.Piggott | 10-1 |
| 1977 | The Minstrel | L.Piggott | 5-1 |
| 1978 | Shirley Heights | G.Starkey | 8-1 |
| 1979 | Troy | W.Carson | 6-1 |

**Epsom High Street in August 1972. The Woolwich Building Society has already moved into the former National Counties Bank premises which, when it amalgamated with the National Westminster, was closed because it would have meant three branches of the bank being situated in the town.**

# Epsom in 1972

After a long controversy in local government, it was decided that Epsom and Ewell should stay within the same boundaries, even though Banstead, after a massive fight, was allowed to merge with Reigate under some of the biggest boundary changes this century.

**January:** Epsom and Ewell householders started the year stocking up with coal during the fuel crisis, in anticipation of the miners' strike. Also in January, suggestions were made that evening horse races should be held on Epsom Downs. Surrey County Council raised West Hill House, Epsom, to the status of "historic interest." In Reid's department store in Epsom, items in the January sale included Playtex pantie girdles for £2.99 each and fitted wardrobes "finished with easy-to-clean white Melamine" at £79.95 each.

**February:** Ewell's St. Mary's Church launched a £30,000 fund to pay for church and hall repairs. A £1.25million sports and leisure centre was mooted for Epsom. Two hundred objections were received against Epsom's town centre and inner relief road scheme. Housewives "watched notices saying when they could cook" because of a strike by electricity power workers. Two recreation grounds — Auriol Park and Court Playing Field, set up "doggie" toilets. The borough's first full-time day centre for elderly people, at The Cedars, in Church Street, Epsom, was established.

**March:** The borough's biggest-ever rate rise — 98.3p in the £ — a jump of 11.2p, was announced. One of Epsom's newest stores, Key Markets, which had opened in 1963, said it was to close down.

**April:** The county council gave the go-ahead for the conversion of West Hill House into flats for 34 elderly people. Epsom's first woman doctor, Dr. Barbara Mitchell, retired. Commuters forced their way into the cab of an Epsom train when a driver refused to take it on to Dorking, during a rail workers' go-slow. A two-week long inquiry into Epsom town centre began. Stoneleigh woman Sylvia Cook, 33, and friend John Fairfax, reached Australia after rowing 8,000 miles across the

**Upper High Street, Epsom, in 1972. The supermarket on the left is Homefare, which became International some years later, then Lipton's and Gateway before closing down in 1994. Other stores on the left include DER electrical and Angelique.**

Pacific Ocean.

**May:** Proposals to close post offices for half a day a week and at lunchtimes, sparked an outcry among traders in Epsom and Banstead.

**June:** Proposals were put forward by the Levy Board to rebuild Epsom grandstand and build an indoor athletics track, tennis courts and other facilities, occupying a bigger area of the downs.

**July:** Sainsbury's closed its shop in Upper High Street, Epsom, after trading in the town for 71 years. An action group of 100 people was formed to fight plans for a gipsy site at Drift Bridge.

**August:** Tragedy struck when two former Ewell Castle schoolboys, John Isard and Maurice Groves, both aged 23, drowned while on a boating holiday in Cornwall. A fire broke out at Ewell Territorial Army Drill Hall, in which two gas cylinders exploded.

Vandals cost Epsom and Ewell Football Club £1,000 a year and intruders started a fire in the new £450,000 extension to Ewell Secondary School, Ruxley Lane. Plans for overspill housing at Horton Farm were halted.

**September:** Epsom's second-hand bookshop, Burl's, in South Street, closed after 42 years of trading. The Bishop of Arundel and Brighton opened an £80,000 St.Clement's First School at Fennell's Road, Ewell.

Traders from all over the area opposed plans for a huge out-of-town shopping centre at Lower Kingswood, which, had it been constructed,would have been called Banstead Heights.

**October:** Epsom Labour Party chose 22-year-old trade union official, Neil Kearney, as a parliamentary prospective candidate.

**November:** Ancillary staff at Long Grove Hospital threatened strike action because of the introduction of a new hours rota.

There was a panic rush to buy candles as the power workers' industrial dispute escalated.

**December:** Epsom and Ewell Council went on record as being in favour of the introduction of stronger powers to prevent the unplanned demolition of properties in the town centre.

O.W. Annetts and Sons, office supplies, Upper High Street, Epsom, in the early 1970s. The Wimpy Bar later became a branch of the Kentucky Fried Chicken fast-food chain.

Coppen's, the draper's, pictured here in about 1971, was later to become FADS. The store traded at the foot of Upper High Street, Epsom.

# Venture Scouts halt trains

TWO Epsom Venture Scouts caused two trains to be halted for three hours, on the Reading-Tonbridge line, by placing a hoax bomb alongside the track, in 1973.

The 'bomb' was part of a night exercise they had devised which it was intended should be found by another team of scouts. However, it was put in the wrong place by a misread map reference.

The two scouts, from the Ashley Venture Unit, were most contrite and did not intend to cause disruption, but said they wanted a topical theme.

A judge ordered them to raise £150, by voluntary work, to pay for the money which had been wasted in the incident.

The Locomotive public house, in East Street, Epsom, had two name changes after this picture was taken in 1971. It first became The Common Room and then, in more recent times, The Bears. The shops in the foreground have long since been demolished to make way for offices.

In 1971, police were called to the derelict Shrubbery, South Street, Epsom, in their Morris 1100 patrol car, after reports that squatters had moved in. The building, which dated back to the 1600s, was demolished in March 1977.

# Cloudburst at Epsom

A "storm of the century" hit Epsom on Wednesday evening, 17th August, 1977. At least one-and-three-quarters of an inch of rain fell. Firemen rescued Miss Enid Pierce, who was nearly drowned when her Mini was swept into five feet of flood water under the railway bridge in West Street. She clambered out of the window and hung on to the side of the car for dear life. Firemen waded through water which was chest-deep, to rescue her.

Front page headlines from the *Sunday Times* dated 18th September 1977, after the East Ewell kidnap victim had been found.

*Joyce McKinney fantasized about victim, it was alleged*

# Kidnap of a Mormon at Ewell

In September 1977 a bizarre event hit the headlines, when a Mormon missionary was kidnapped in Ewell. Kirk Anderson, 21, disappeared on Wednesday, 14th September, from outside the Church of Jesus Christ of Latter Day Saints, in Banstead Road, opposite the large playing fields. The incident sparked off a massive police hunt.

He was eventually released, unharmed, near Victoria Station, in London. He rang Scotland Yard police to say he had been kidnapped and held handcuffed and manacled for three days - apparently on the orders of a wealthy, love-sick woman.

Anderson told police he would get a train back to Epsom, so he could return to his home in Milton Gardens, but he boarded the wrong train and ended up at Sutton Station. He contacted police again and they collected him.

He told police of long talks with his captors also about his relationship with a former girlfriend in Salt Lake City, the Mormon Church's global headquarters.

He said he had had a blanket thrown over his head and that he had been driven, for four to five hours, to a house he did not know. Although he had been handcuffed, and his legs chained together, he told police he had been well-fed and looked after.

Detective Chief Superintendent Bill Hucklesbury, at Epsom, who headed the search for Anderson, told reporters: "This seems to be the case of hell hath no fury like a woman scorned. We have her name and are now trying to establish, together with the FBI, whether she is in this country."

It is believed that Anderson was taken to a cottage on the remote edge of Dartmoor and chained to a bed. On the Monday following his release, an American former beauty queen, Miss Joyce McKinney, a Mormon, was held by police after her car was stopped in Devon, at a police road block. She was then taken to Epsom Police Station, together with four men.

Anderson had arrived in this country the previous year, from Provo in Utah, USA.

Joyce McKinney escaped the clutches of the police and fled to Ireland and then America and, 20 years after this extraordinary episode, there was still a warrant out for her arrest, according to police at Epsom.

McKinney allegedly confessed she was obsessed with Anderson and it was reported in the tabloid press that she would have skiied naked down a mountain, with a red rose, if it meant she could have her man.

Commuters, at East Ewell Station, board the 8.20am Southern Region Dorking to Victoria train, on 25th April 1973.

A Ewell housewife waits for the washing to finish at the Washeteria in Ewell High Street.

The Glyn Arms, Cheam Road, Ewell, in July 1973. In the next decade the name changed to TJs and the premises became an American-style burger restaurant pub.

*An unsolved murder at Effingham*

# Some notable crimes

One of Surrey's few unsolved murder cases, in recent times, is that of Maude Cock, an elderly widow who lived in Effingham. On the night of Wednesday, 26th November, 1975, Mrs Cock was killed in her own home at Surrey Gardens. She had been beaten around the head at least a dozen times and was left to die in a pool of blood. Her wedding ring had been removed from her finger.

Despite extensive enquiries over the years, the culprit had not been caught.

It is thought that five-feet-tall, Mrs Cock, who lived alone, may have let someone who was known to her into her home, because there did not appear to have been a struggle.

**Murder victim, Mrs Maude Cock.**

On the day of the 78-year-old's death it is known she caught the train to Guildford, from Effingham Junction, to do some shopping. A week later police interviewed dozens of passengers on the line, in the hope of gaining clues as to her exact movements on that fateful day.

Some 20 years later, Surrey Police were still hoping that new evidence would come to light.

Two years after Mrs Cock's death, Coulsdon was shocked by the brutal murder of Mrs Joy Sweatman, at her home in St. Andrew's Road, Coulsdon, on Derby Day, 1977.

The crime remained unsolved for years.

---

## £433,000 raid

On 1st April, 1973, in a raid on Twickenham head post office, thieves escaped with cash and stamps worth £433,000.

## Schoolboy killed

A 14-year-old schoolboy died at Sutton west High School, Sutton, after he was stabbed in a classroom fight (See Sutton and Cheam chapter, page 55).

## Aldershot bomb

An IRA man was jailed for life on 14th October, 1972, for planting a bomb outside the Parachute Regiment's Officers mess, at Aldershot, on 22nd February 1972. It exploded, killing five women domestic workers, a civilian gardener and a chaplain. A number of them were injured. The London bomb outrages occurred between 21st and 23rd August, 1971.

## Kidnap of Muriel McKay

On 6th October, 1970, two brothers, Arthur and Nizamodeen Hosein, were sentenced to life imprisonment for murdering Mrs Muriel McKay, after kidnapping her from her home in Arthur Road, Wimbledon, and taking her to their Essex farmhouse where they demanded a £1million ransom. Her body was never found.

---

# Garage killing at Burgh Heath

A former popular Chessington and Tolworth milkman, Bill Melvin, 51, a night cashier at a Burgh Heath petrol station was beaten to death in an early hours raid on 18th September 1976.

**Bill Melvin**

A 19-year-old labourer, and a 29-year-old demolition worker who lived in Hillside Close, Nork, Banstead, were later charged with murder but were convicted of manslaughter.

Each received a jail term of nearly ten years. The robbery happened at Auto Sales and Services Garage in Brighton Road.

Above: a tinder-dry railway embankment, at The Fairfield, Farnham, went up in flames on 23rd August, 1976, setting fire to a warehouse and a house. Above right: Farnham firemen, and a British Rail official, discuss the serious fire situation at the location.

## *Flames sweep Surrey countryside*

# The long, hot summer of '76

Sizzling sunshine, rivers running dry, ponds disappearing, trees wilting and crops failing. 'Share a bath with a friend and save water,' was one solution offered by a national newspaper.

No-one would forget the summer of 1976, which brought the most memorable drought and prolonged heat, arguably of all time, and Surrey looked more like Southern Spain, by mid-August, than the more usual verdant vista characterized by one of Britain's most wooded counties.

Temperatures topped 95F (35C) from Guildford to Ewell and in the Staines area, 21 days saw the mercury above 86F (30C) with 38 consecutive rainless days in Guildford. There was no relief for Surrey commuters, working in the capital, because few buildings had air-conditioning, and many travellers suffered from heat exhaustion on crowded trains, as did hundreds of spectators at the Wimbledon tennis championships.

The heat, and prolonged drought, which had been exacerbated by the previous dry winter, took its toll on the countryside, as thousands of acres went up in flames with over 11,000 calls to the Surrey Fire Brigade, and a familiar sight was the Home Office Green Goddess pumping appliances which were called in to help the embattled fire service. One of the most serious outbreaks was near Tilford, where a frightening wall of flame raced through the trees, forcing local residents to flee for their lives. Over 50 paratroopers, from Aldershot and 20 policemen from Farnham, joined the fire brigade to help quell the inferno.

The widespread nature of the fires was very well illustrated by Chris Hall, in the *Farnham Herald*, who wrote about his journey across the Surrey/Hampshire border. He saw eight separate columns of smoke. A fire at Thursley had split into three, raging across the common. There were two fires on Ash Ranges, two from the Deepcut direction and one from Hook Common, and everywhere smoke and ash gave a lurid glow to the sky and an acrid smell to the air.

Nor was the east and north of Surrey spared. A woman dialled 999 when woodland started blazing at Claygate, but she was told, point blank, that no engine could attend. Nearly 200 fires a day were raging and Surrey Fire Brigade H.Q. even had to bring in extra staff to man the telephone lines. Eventually an appliance from Reigate, carrying trainee firemen, pulled in at Littleworth Common to quell the flames. Meanwhile another fire caused a huge pall of smoke to hang over Surbiton, when five acres of tinder dry grass was caught ablaze at Lower Marsh Lane. Forest fires swept Esher's countryside, too.

**The 1975 summer was also noted for the heat. This was the *Woking News and Mail*, on 7th August, 1975.**

**Chobham firemen turn out, in 1975. They were kept very busy in both 1975 and 1976, tackling many grass and woodland fires.**

An inferno sped across Walton Heath and co-author of this book, Ian Currie, remembers this because he was blackberrying near The Sportsman public house at Mogador. Looking north, billowing smoke was swept by a strong north-east breeze, across the common. A fire had leapt across the Dorking Road, threatening properties near the road and at Walton-on-the-Hill. The flame front extended for two miles and some 50 firemen fought all afternoon, in beating down the flames and making firebreaks. Flames scorched two houses on the heath before firemen arrived, just in time, to save them.

A sign of how serious the situation had become, was the forlorn sight of an empty reservoir at Bough Beech, which supplies water to East Surrey, and for the first time in recorded history, Burgh Heath Pond completely dried up, creating huge cracks and fissures, as the natural springs failed, killing the fish and driving away the bird life.

Even the River Mole ran dry, with not a trickle of water to be seen at Young Street, Leatherhead. For the first time, since 1940, East Surrey Water Company had to force people to save water and imposed a hosepipe and car wash ban and the local branch of the National Hairdressers' Federation urged folk to save water by reducing the time taken to shampoo, using a spray and only having one wash and rinse.

Teachers conducted lessons under the shade of spreading oaks, at de Stafford School, Caterham, and security guards were hired to keep bathers out of British Industrial Sand's water-filled quarries in Merstham. Hundreds of bathers flocked there to cool off and the secluded spot became a nudists' paradise. Meanwhile, shops in Croydon, ran out of T-shirts.

Two small boys were shocked to see what appeared to be a body floating on Frensham Little Pond. Immediately the police were called to carry out what could have been a gruesome discovery, and out they rowed. However, to their surprise, they found a rubber dummy, half submerged, which had been thrown into the pond in 1969, during the filming of Lost Valley, starring Michael Caine. The water level had dropped 27 inches, revealing the missing figure.

**A reservoir, near Walton-on-Thames, dried out after the 1976 heatwave.**

**Allders' store in Croydon advertised the latest fashions, in January 1974.**

**The 1970s saw the worst labour relations since the General Strike in 1926. The queue in the picture above, formed because there was a shortage of bread, due to strikes in the bakers' unions at the flour mills. Queues of people, in a desperate search for the elusive loaf, extended along the High Street, in Croydon, on 6th December, 1974.**

## *Rubbish piles up in the streets; bloated flies fall into pub beer*

# Croydon goes on strike

Croydonians shivered and spluttered into the new decade. They were victims of a wintry start to 1970 and to an influenza epidemic which swept through the borough.

Over 10,000 people were sick with 'flu during the first week and 18 people died as hospitals were put on red alert and told only to accept emergency cases. At Mayday, Thornton Heath, volunteers were asked to help out as up to 100 nurses were ill.

Influenza delayed a selection meeting for a prospective Parliamentary candidate to the constituency of Croydon Northwest, which was being vacated by Mr Fred Harris in this year's election, the one in which 18-year-olds would be voting for the first time. It was also cited as an excuse for reckless driving at the Arkwright Roundabout, Sanderstead, when a lady repeatedly rammed her car against a tree. She was somewhat inebriated and said that her drinking was helping her to combat the 'flu.

A thick snowstorm enveloped Croydon during the morning of Thursday 12th February. Cars were abandoned on Gravel Hill and in the Selsdon area; de-icing trains were running round-the-clock through East Croydon Station and snow lay on the ground for eight days. Another snowstorm struck in early March and at one point 13 buses were stuck on the four to five inches of snow on Sanderstead Hill. The temperature fell to 20F(-7C).

Bad weather and the 'flu epidemic were blamed as causes for a shortage of smokeless fuel, stated the head of the National Coal Board, Lord Robbins, a Woldingham resident. Britain was short of 700,000 tons of smokeless fuel. Croydon's gas works had been converted to using oil, instead of coal, and the borough lost a source of coke as a by-product. There was a clamour to rescind the Clean Air Act which entailed a £20 fine for those people using the wrong fuel.

A scream probably saved a little boy's life. A young lad was walking home from Gilbert Scott Infant School when curiosity overcame him as he

**Looking down on the Whitgift Centre, Croydon, open to the elements, in early July 1972. Overcoats were certainly needed when the temperatures failed to rise above 57F (14C) on this day.**

passed the workings of the new Monks Hill Secondary School. He slipped down a bank into the path of a tipper truck unloading tons of wet, sandy earth. A lady happened to see the boy fall and screamed and hollered at the driver to stop pouring. It was not a second too soon as the infant was already buried up to his armpits. The driver responded to the screams and the boy was rescued.

There were two innovations in the spring. Dial-a-Disc came to Croydon. From 6pm to 8am, and all day on Sunday, callers could dial 160 and for 6d (2!/2p), could listen to the latest records from the Top Twenty, such as "Bridge Over Troubled Water" by Simon and Garfunkel, "Wand'rin Star" by Lee Marvin, "Spirit In The Sky" by Norman Greenbaum or "Back Home," by the England World Cup Squad. A different hit was selected each day. There were 2,000 calls in just 10 days. There was less enthusiasm for one-man operated buses which were first used on the 'C' routes from Croydon to New Addington. Complaints ranged

from them being too slow, that they often broke down, they lacked comfort or the stops were not convenient. A *Croydon Advertiser* reporter recounted his journey, saying that it took eight minutes from West to East Croydon in the rush hour. The vehicle was stationary for one minute ten seconds whilst passengers queued to put their 1s 6d in the fare box and the bus took 34 minutes to get to Homestead Way. Delays occurred because the automatic doors failed to open and had to be manually operated.

A Croydon dog, Abel Mabel, was the mother of Winston, the mascot for England's World cup football team who were about to set off for Mexico. Winston brought them luck until the quarter finals when they were knocked out by West Germany after being two goals to nil in front.

The first week of May gave predominantly fine weather, with the temperature climbing to a summer-like 70F (21C). It was time to relax in the garden and enjoy the first real settled weather of the spring. Soon, though, residents were scurry-

**A fine Saturday in early June, 1977, and shoppers were out in force in a non-pedestrianised Croydon High Street. Unfortunately the fine weather was not to last for the Queen's Silver Jubilee, a few days later. The decorations seen on Allders department store were to become quite wet by the end of the Royal day.**

ing back indoors to escape what was described by many as "a strong pong." The beastly odour, likened to horse manure, hung in the air over Croydon. Traffic wardens fled their offices in Mitcham Road. Stores in George Street kept their doors closed and the stench spoilt the jollities of Mitcham Fair and was nauseating in Waddon. It wafted as far as Sanderstead. Croydon Council disclaimed responsibility, so did the gasworks and it was not long before the sewage farm at Beddington became the chief suspect. Untreated sludge had been spread in the open air as the tanks were being cleaned and the strong sunshine heightened the stench.

The sludge was eventually covered with deodorant, lime and earth. However, the smell proved more belligerent than the staff thought, and the problem really was about outmoded and inadequate Edwardian apparatus, particularly as Croydon's population had grown considerably since then. New tanks were approved, at an overall cost of £1million to the Greater London Council.

Good weather traditionally helps Labour in voting terms but it did not assist them in the General Election this year as the Conservatives swept the board within the borough.

King Charles II spoke of the English summer as comprising: "three fine days and a thunderstorm." A brief hot spell broke down in dramatic fashion during the evening of 7th July, after temperatures had reached 87F (31C), at Waddon and 85F (29C) in Addington. Lightning struck five houses, including two in Fosse Way, Waddon, where 10 children were sleeping. Debris came crashing down from the ceiling, showering a two-year-old in a cot. Her mother had just closed the bedroom window to stop the rain from coming in. The terrified mum dashed into the room again to find the cot covered in dust and debris and four other children were cowering under a table with the dog. Luckily the children escaped injury. Another house, in Harcourt Road, Thornton Heath, had a huge hole punched in its roof. Another storm, during the morning of 6th August, flooded the centre of Croydon. At Allders, 17 departments were flooded as nearly an inch of rain fell. Water was waist deep by the fire escape between W.H.Smith's and Allders. There were 30 calls to the fire brigade including one from a

**Croydon High Street, bedecked with Silver Jubilee bunting, in late May 1977, as the town prepared for the festivities in early June.**

ladies' hairdresser in Stanley Road. Five women were under the drying machines just as a torrent of water rushed in. Machines were hastily unplugged, to avoid a nasty shock, and the ladies waded out of the door and made their way to another premises in South Norwood, for their hair-dos to be completed.

At least it remained dry for a fun day at Ashburton Park, which attracted 14,000 visitors. One popular, but curious sideshow, was that of having the chance to be a dentist. All the instruments a dentist uses were on display together with a rubber head, complete with a set of teeth. The latter came in for quite a hammering, during the afternoon, from queues of eager children wanting to have a go at extracting.

For a number of families, the Seventies was a time of uncertainty as the prospect loomed of a full-blown motorway forging its way through suburbia. An orbital motorway was proposed, encircling London and scything through Norbury, North Croydon and with not even Selhurst Park, home of Crystal Palace F.C. being safe. Hundreds of homes were blighted, but in spite of this, major building work was planned for Stanley Technical School, South Norwood Hill. The school must not be cursed by indecision, according to the Chief Education Officer, and £73,000 was allocated to expansion, including a sixth form for 60 boys.

A survey of Croydon's roads revealed that there were 12,000 holes, some of which were unexplained. Manor, Wiltshire and Warwick Roads all had holes, some of which had been there for two years! A borough engineer stated that utility companies were not informing the council of their plans, nor when they had completed work, in order that roads and pavements could be made good.

The year of 1970 was to prove the most strike-torn since the General Strike in 1926. Prices of meat, in Croydon shops, were reported to have risen by as much as up to 6d a pound for lamb, because of a national dock strike. Businesses in the borough were affected, one of the most prominent being Holt products, car and motor accessories, which had £50,000-worth of goods on strike-bound ships. Waves of strikes affected Britain later in the year but in August, figures were released showing that unemployment was less than one per cent within Croydon.

**An RM 119A bus to West Croydon and an M-reg Ford Cortina, travel past the Allders store in Croydon, in May 1977.**

At a council meeting in October, a proposal was accepted for a six-day trading week, rather than observing the requirements of the 1950 Shops Act which meant shops closing early one day during the week as well as on Sunday. Now a freedom of choice was given to stay open but the big stores, such as Grants and Allders, expressed concern that extra wage bills could exceed £20,000 to £30,000 per annum.

Industrial unrest intensified during the autumn as council manual workers went on strike thus affecting refuse collection, sewage treatment, highways, school bus drivers and even crematorium employees. On a national scale, power workers, the fire brigade and ambulance drivers were working to rule.

Power cuts played havoc with daily life. Cars, lorries and buses came to a halt as traffic lights failed, people were trapped in lifts, factories lost production and Croydon's old age pensioners were advised to stay in bed in order to keep warm. The British Home Stores lost £2,000 an hour in business. Fairfield Hall abandoned its stage presen-

tation of "The Amorous Prawn" but the most graphic headline was reserved for the massive piles of rubbish which were appearing on nearly every street, leading to a description of the borough as a "land where bloated flies are the lords." Several pub landlords said they constantly had to give customers extra pints because flies kept landing in their drinks. One old age pensioner spent all day shovelling into piles, bad meat, rotten vegetables and fruit, which lined Purley Downs Road, and then later burned them.

The strike was for 55 shillings a week extra to add to their basic grade of £13.15s.0d and 35 shillings was offered. Eventually 50 shillings was proposed, and accepted, with overtime payments to clear up the mess.

One casualty of the strikes was Famet Close, Purley, where, for many years, residents had fought to have the road adopted so as to be released from the seasonal perils of thick, cloying mud and immense lakes. Just as work started it came to a halt, as did that on many other road schemes throughout the borough. Bad though

# Metric never, yards forever

**Mr Barry Bond, and his father, Harry, campaigned under the slogan: "Metric Never, Yards Forever." The father and son team had run Bonds draper's shop in Church Street, for 25 years, and were alarmed at the confusion that metrification was causing amongst their customers. They instigated a petition, in the spring of 1978, which soon had 500 signatures.**

our problems were, they paled into insignificance compared with the horrendous conditions in Bangladesh and India where up to a million people died in a powerful cyclone.

Within a few days the borough had raised £1,000, including £53 from Benson Primary School, and nationally Sir Richard Attenborough launched the appeal which soon raised £1,303,170 for the stricken countries.

On a lighter note, the Whitgift Centre received a visit from the Duchess of Kent and 3,000 shoppers and office workers were on hand to greet her. The *Croydon Advertiser* described her fashion sense as impeccable, from her touches of white to her chunky-heeled shoes.

Croydon experienced a rare white Christmas, with parks and gardens looking as pretty as the most festive of cards. Up to six inches of snow fell but one family was not impressed. A lady, in Shirley, slipped and broke her leg while she was delivering presents.

An ambulance was called and it promptly became stuck in the snow, and had to be dug out, as it made its way to Mayday Hospital.

Another casualty was the Boxing Day football derby between Crystal Palace and Chelsea, but the wintry conditions did not seem to daunt the spirit of bargain hunters at the New Year Allders' sales. Long queues formed early, waiting for the shop doors to open.

Purley shops in about 1972 - minus the usual traffic.

A 725 Green Line coach, destined for Windsor, leaves West Croydon bus station in April 1972, en route to Sutton and Kingston. Behind it is a 405 green bus to Crawley, via Redhill.

**A busy scene at Purley Cross during 1975.**

**St. Ann's College, Sanderstead, viewed from Heath Hurst Road in the late 1970s, before it was demolished.**

*Foxes unearthed woman's arm*

# Leatherhead golf course murder case

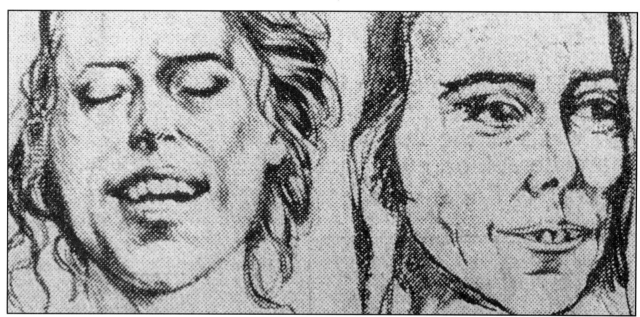

**An artist's impression of how the woman may have looked.**

Foxes in the woods at Leatherhead unearthed an arm of a woman, sparking a gruesome murder enquiry in the late summer of 1971.

The grim discovery was made by a man playing an early evening round of golf on the course beside the A243, south of Chessington Zoo.

Fetcham dentist Dennis O'Flyn and golfing pal, Michael Fisher, of Little Bookham, were enjoying a round on Wednesday 1st September when Mr.O'Flyn's ball went into the rough. A few moments later he exclaimed to Mr.Fisher: "I've found an arm!" On closer inspection it was found to be a forearm and hand, with two rings on the fingers. It was in a bad state of decomposition.

There followed a huge murder enquiry, led by one of Scotland Yard's brightest detectives, Det. Chief Supt. Peter Shemming, who had solved 10 murders in East London. He moved to the Bookham Grange Hotel so as to be near the incident room at Leatherhead Police Station. Among the officers helping him in the investigation was Detective Chief Insp. Philip Doyle, who three years earlier had headed the investigation into the murder of Brockham schoolboy, Roy Tutill, which remains unsolved.

**Police remove the remains from the 18-inch deep grave, where parts of the body were found wrapped in plastic and buried under a sapling oak tree.**

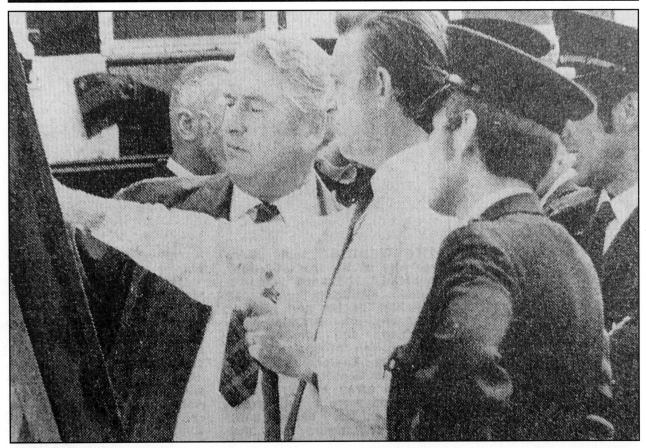

Police led by Det. Chief Insp. Philip Doyle are briefed before they begin to search for parts of a woman's body on Leatherhead golf course in September 1971.

Michael Fisher (above) of Little Bookham, was playing golf with a friend, who made the grim discovery of a woman's arm in the rough.

Headlines from the *Leatherhead Advertiser* days later.

**Headlines from the *Leatherhead Advertiser* after the accused man is led to court in Epsom.**

As soon as the arm was discovered, a thorough search of the nearby copses was made. The detectives were aided by a tramp, who lived in a ramshackle shelter in the woods—the hermit, Ted "Old Bill" Churcher, who had lived rough in Rowhurst Woods, off the Oxshott Road, for 30 years. He knew the woods intimately and immediately led police to a grave, after he had been asked to pinpoint any spot where soil may have been disturbed.

Using a slasher — a long handle with a blade attached — he prodded a small ridge of soil near the ninth green and found pieces came away easily, indicating to him that the soil had been dug in the not-too-distant past. He prised away some humus to reveal a plastic bag which contained the torso. He saw that the arms had also been severed and he told the police that the head had been cut cleanly from the torso by an axe or similar tool.

Helped by Godstone fox expert, Pc Pat Buss, a search was made for other limbs. Curiously, both left-side limbs were placed in a holdall, in the same grave, near the tenth fairway, which showed "an unusual neatness on the part of the killer."

Using two specially-trained collie dogs from Lancashire, the golf course was combed for the other right-side limbs — a leg below the knee, a foot and an upper arm. Part of a forearm was found in bracken by Pc Buss and the other remains were found in two further shallow graves close by.

While 60 police searched the thickets, 70 women golfers took part in an invitation match on the course, just yards away.

The head was later found nearby. It was wrapped in a copy of the *Evening Standard* dated 5th December 1968, but it was the dead woman's teeth, in the skull, which gave police their biggest clue.

Forensic tests showed that the victim was clad in a slip and chainstore "shortie" housecoat. The slip was of an unusual design, with a zip at the back. One of the legs found had on the foot a size three cheap blue corduroy slipper, with thick com-

**The victim, Mrs Elenora Essens.**

**Red roses for woman he killed**

**Census shows town's slow growth**

FOXES foraging for food near Leatherhead Golf Course unearthed the dismembered body of a woman murdered nearly three years earlier, said Mr Richard Lowry, QC, prosecuting at the Old Bailey on Monday.

Alexander Leonard Vanags, 44, a Latvian-born book editor of Sut-

Vanags said he took the parts of the body by bus and train to Leatherhead Golf Course and buried them. Earlier he had bought red roses

THE POPULATION the Leatherhead dist has gone up by nea 5,000 in 11 years. 1971 census figures

**Headlines from the trial reported in the _Leatherhead Advertiser_ in July 1972.**

position sole. The woman's hair was dark brown, with strands of grey at the front and it grew to neck level. It was straight, except for a slight curl at the temples. Tests also showed she had undergone a hysterectomy operation.

As part of their appeal for information, broadcasts were made by the police on the forecourt of The Star public house, Leatherhead Road, Chessington.

In addition, appeals were made on TV's Police Five, presented by Shaw Taylor and to 30,000 dentists across the country. The dental records had to be thoroughly searched at every surgery, said Chief Supt. Shemming, who was deputy head of criminal intelligence at Scotland Yard.

At first it was thought that the body may be that of Muriel McKay, abducted by the Hosein brothers from her home in Arthur Road, Wimbledon, or the body of Mrs Kathleen Tipton, of Wallington, whose husband was serving five years in jail for her manslaughter.

Increasingly, following the publication of an artist's impression in the press and the dental details in trade journals, evidence pointed towards the Mansfield area of Nottinghamshire.

In November of 1971 there was a dramatic breakthrough, when a dentist positively identified the dental records as those of Mrs Elenora Essens. Mrs Essens turned out to be a 50-year-old Latvian, formerly of Mansfield, last seen at Christmas 1968, in Chiswick. She had earlier lived with a man in a flat at Cheam. Mrs Essens' husband, coalminer Alexander Essens, still lived in the Mansfield home she had left in 1965. The couple had been seen frequently at dances run by

the Latvian Welfare Association, in Mansfield. They had met when both were in a German labour camp during the Second World War and Mrs.Essens is thought to have had two children, who died in Europe. Mr and Mrs Essens were married with the silver ring made by a friend and which helped Mr Essens to identify the Leatherhead murder victim as his wife. In London, Mr Essens was said to have been friendly with the Greek community.

Positive identification was also secured when Mr Essens contacted Det. Chief Spt. Shemming after seeing the Police Five TV programme on Saturday 13th November. Two hundred people rang the incident room following the programme.

The naming of the victim on 19th November also led to a dramatic development. A man who lived with Mrs Essens at Chiswick came forward and told police he had killed her.

Latvian-born editor of technical books, Aleksander Leonard Vanags, aged 44, of Sutton Lane, Chiswick, appeared before Epsom Magistrates on Wednesday 12th January 1972, charged with the murder of Mrs Elenora Essens. The stockily-built man appeared in the dock wearing a blue-grey suit, white shirt and grey tie and stood with his arms folded as the charges were read to him. He made no reply. He had been taken to the court from Dorking Police Station, where he had been kept overnight.

After the brief hearing, he was led to a K-registration police car, with his head under a blanket. At his trial at the Old Bailey in July 1972, he was sentenced to three years' jail for manslaughter. The court heard how, just after Christmas 1968,

**Detective Chief Superintendent Peter Shemming (right) and his assistant, Detective Sergeant Robin Constable, who lived at Banstead, holding gifts presented to them by detectives of Surrey Constabulary. The two men formed part of a 35-man team working on the Leatherhead golf course murder investigation.**

Mrs Essens and Vanags had a terrible row at their flat in Chiswick. She had provoked him by saying he was "no good in bed." He replied that was because she had "ruined his nerves." In a rage, she had torn up his technical books, telling him he was more interested in his books than he was in her. He had tried to restrain her, but she seemed hell-bent on destroying his work.

In the heat of the moment, he had grabbed an unloaded German gas pistol and struck her several times on the back of the head. She fell to the ground, unconscious. He listened for her heartbeat, but it was non-existent.

After three or four days, with his brain in turmoil, he set about removing the body. Drowning his emotions with half a bottle of vodka and with his eyes closed, he used a hacksaw to cut off her head, then he later severed the limbs. He put the head in a cardboard box and tied it up with string. Then he took the boxed head, by tube, to a left luggage department at Victoria Station. He placed the limbs in plastic bags and also left them in lockers.

When Vanags returned to the station, to his consternation he found the box containing the head had vanished from the locker. Staff at the station had removed the box after the time limit

had expired, but he was able to retrieve it from a storeroom. Vanags told police he took the remains by train and bus to Leatherhead golf course, to bury them. It is believed that the bus he used was the Green Line 714 Kingston to Dorking service. He got off the bus at the Pachesham Park gates near The Star public house and set about burying the packages.

In each of the shallow graves he placed a red rose "because I loved her." He also used a penknife to carve the initial "N" in the young oak tree under which he buried his lover. He said he had hoped to return at a later date to "give her a decent burial."

The jury considered there were grounds for reducing the charge to manslaughter and Vanags admitted causing her death on or about 29th December 1968 and burying her remains. The Old Bailey Judge praised Det. Chief Supt. Shemming for solving what was nearly the "undetectable crime."

At a ceremony which followed, Mr. Shemming was presented with gifts from Surrey Police in appreciation of his efforts. Two weeks later Mr. Shemming retired from the force, to manage a large country club in Essex, partly owned by Sean Connery, alias James Bond.

An advertisement in the *Leatherhead Advertiser* for the VG Supermarket, in Great Bookham, in February 1973.

## *Mungo Jerry and Desmond Dekker play at youth centre*

# Flowery flares in Bookham

Bookham was a typical Surrey village in the Seventies and it had a strong sense of community. Among the shops in the centre was Brackenbury's, a hardware store, which used to be three shops wide until the advent of out-of-town DIY superstores, and garden centres, cut its trade and it was forced to reduce to a single unit. Capel's the greengrocer's, used to trade in Church Street, and vegetables would be sold by the manager who had a distinctive sideburns. This shop was later moved to the main road.

One young mother, Mrs Ann Cattermole, recalled going to the shops with her new baby, Sarah, who was pushed in a navy blue Silver Cross high carriage pram.

She parked the baby outside John Suffolk's VG store in High Street, Great Bookham, and when she came out with her provisions she forgot all about little Sarah!

"I went home without her. I just wasn't used to thinking about prams and toddlers," Mrs Cattermole recollected years later. "I went back and she was lying there, as good as gold. She had

been there for half-an-hour."

Ann also remembered keeping up with the latest fashions. "We used to cut 10 inches off the bottom of our jeans and put a flowery bit of material in the flares. Later on we made our daughters flowery reversible waistcoats to go with their flares."

In the Royal Oak there was no canned music then, apparently, but around 1969-70, there were some lively scenes at Bookham Youth Centre, opposite to the Anchor public house. Built in 1968, by the council, for the village's youngsters, a thriving social scene emerged from the youth centre.

Pop groups, which drew large crowds, were booked, and among the acts which villagers say played there, were Mungo Jerry and Desmond Dekker. The club was run by the dynamic John Hyde, who booked these acts long before they climbed to the top of the charts.

However, despite becoming famous in the meantime, they still kept their long-standing bookings at the club.

*Experimental one-way system around town*

# Leatherhead in 1971-72

Planners introduced an experimental one-way system around Leatherhead town centre in the summer of 1971, but the scheme met with strong opposition and in September, 30 pram-pushing mums rolled up at the Leatherhead Council Offices to object.

They handed the Town Clerk, Mr L.A.Stray, a petition containing 1,500 signatures from people opposed to the traffic system.

In conjunction with Leatherhead Residents' Association, the action group presented to the council their own version of a one-way system, which they contended would be better for the people of the town.

Meanwhile a group of traders, residents and property developers, worried about the future of the shopping area, drew up their own plan for one side of the High Street. They feared that unless Leatherhead Council took action, the hub would become a ghost town of empty shops. Their plan for the eastern side of the High Street, approaching from Ashstead, included shops, with flats above, and a wide, pedestrianised area. The plan had the blessing of Boots, Sainsbury's, B.S.C. Footwear and Thorn Electrics.

An alternative plan was for two sets of shops with separate pedestrian precincts. A multi-storey car park, or two-storey block, was also included in the plan.

The shopping precinct idea had been prepared by the Leatherhead Property Trust, part of a large London combine run by the Reeves family who once lived in The Mansion and had long-standing associations with Leatherhead. It was this trust which redeveloped the Thorndike Theatre and Church Street. It had owned the Crescent Cinema before this became the Thorndike Theatre.

A decade later the Swan Centre was emerging and much of the town centre was to be pedestrianised. At the beginning of 1970, the year Edward Heath became the new Conservative Prime Minister, Leatherhead district had a population of about 39,000.

Leatherhead Urban District Council's chairman was A.E.Yearly and the clerk was L.A.Stray.

In May 1971, the *Daily Mail* appeared in Leatherhead's newsagents for the last time as a

**"Spacehoppers" were all the rage in 1969-1970.**

broadsheet. On 3rd May it became a tabloid. A week later the *Daily Sketch*, Britain's oldest tabloid newspaper, closed down.

In Leatherhead's shops, life went on. In September 1971, Barbara Ann hair fashions, in Church Street, Leatherhead (telephone 2172), offered permanent waving from just £2.50 and senior citizens could have a shampoo and set for only 47½p or a cut for 25p. A competitor, Charmaine, in The Crescent, retaliated with a slogan: "Let the beautiful shades of autumn reflect in your hair..."

Parents getting their children prepared for the autumn term could buy canvas satchels from Taylor's for 52p or leather types for £2.50. Tuck boxes, trunks and suitcases were also advertised as well as duffel bags.

The store also took front page advertisement space in the *Leatherhead Advertiser* to draw attention to their cycle dynamos which were on offer at £2.25 (Chopper models £2.40).

Scalextric model car racing sets and Waddington's Monopoly, Careers, Risk, Go and Buccaneer games were also popular lines.

*Plant a tree in '73, plant some more in '74*

# Dutch Elm Disease

The elm tree had for centuries been a part of the English countryside but in the 1970s, Dutch Elm Disease was to change the appearance of Surrey's scenery.

In November 1975, the Forestry Commission reported that more than half the elms in the country had fallen prey to the condition.

Out of 579,000 elms in Surrey, some 300,000 were either dying or had recently died. Another 140,000 had been dead for some time.

In the South of England, as a whole, a further two million elms had been affected in 1975. In the previous year 3.7 million elms in the south, had died but by 1975 the total was estimated to be 5.6 million.

The disease first took hold in the late 1960s and by the 1970s had spread with alarming ease. The hot summers of both 1975 and 1976 only served to exacerbate the problem, the Forestry Commission said.

The Tree Council, formed in 1973 by Surrey County Council, for the Plant A Tree In '73 campaign, was so distressed by the elms situation that it planted a tree a week in 1976.

In October 1975 it was reported that half of the 10,000 elm trees in Kingston Borough, were either dead or dying.

As well as the Plant A Tree In '73 project, there was a follow-up initiative, Plant Some More In '74, and during the drought the next year came the message Keep Them Alive In '75.

## Trains brought in 2,000 frogs a week

Newdigate firm, Gerrard Haig Ltd., made the news in 1975 for its curious importing practices. Some 2,000 common frogs were delivered weekly, from Ireland. Apparently the common frog was scarce in this country.

The frogs came by boat and train to Dorking. They were then picked up by a lorry. The firm then exported the frogs all over Europe, and the world. Were the frogs a delicacy? No, the reason for their popularity was that they were the best for medical experiments.

Customers included Harvard University in America. Business was said to be going ahead by leaps and bounds.

## Leatherhead's soccer stars

One Surrey football team made big headlines in January 1975. Little Isthmian League Club side, Leatherhead, went on to an historic cup run that surprised the football world.

Having already beaten Brighton and Colchester, the team travelled to First Division side, Leicester, for a place in the quarter-finals on 31st January.

Not many experts gave the part-timers from Surrey much hope, but plumber, Peter McGillicuddy and upholsterer, Chris Kelly, put the Surrey side two-nil up. Unfortunately for Leatherhead, as the game went on, the superior fitness of the first division outfit began to tell and the final score was 3-2 to Leicester whose manager, Jimmy Bloomfield, said: "It was a miracle that we won."

Leatherhead's fairy-tale run came to an end in front of over 32,000 fans, including 5,000 who had made the trip from Surrey.

# The Guildford pub bombings

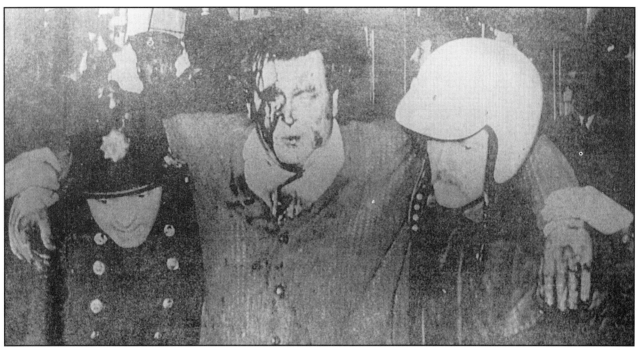

**Injured landlord of The Seven Stars, Swan Lane, Guildford, Mr Brian O'Brien, is led from his pub by rescuers.**

**How the *Surrey Daily Advertiser* reported the bomb horrors.**

On the night of 5th October 1974, Guildford experienced its darkest hour. Two bombs, allegedly planted by IRA terrorists, were placed in two town centre pubs.

The Horse and Groom explosion, in North Street, occurred while the bars were packed with people, enjoying the weekend. Five people were killed and 65 were injured. The huge blast created a hole in the floor, through which some drinkers fell into the cellar, their faces and limbs covered in blood. Some managed to scramble through the piles of bricks and mortar into the street, to get help. The air was full of shouting and screaming. Blood poured down the roads as the injured emerged or were pulled free. The whole of the front of the building caved in.

It was at around 8.50 pm that the Horse and Groom explosion occurred. The second explosion was at the nearby Seven Stars, in Swan Lane, 35 minutes later. It caused extensive interior damage. The pub had been evacuated after the earlier blast up the road. Publican Brian O'Brien, his wife and seven members of staff, plus a girl walking past outside, were injured.

The dead included 18-year-old William Forsyth, of The Guards Depot, Pirbright, John Hunter, aged 17, of the same depot, Anne Hamilton, 18, of Stoughton Barracks, Guildford,

**Clearing up after the explosion the previous night, at The Horse and Groom, North Street, Guildford.**

Caroline Jean Slater, 17, also of Stoughton Barracks and Paul Craig, 22., of Borehamwood, Herts.

Guildford's mayor and mayoress and hundreds of other people were at the nearby civic hall, watching Vernon Handley take applause when the explosions occurred.

An announcement had been made that a "serious accident" had happened in the town centre and that people should avoid the area. The show continued, with the constant sounds of ambulance sirens penetrating the hall.

Many young people from Guildford, Burpham and Merrow were detained at the Royal Surrey Hospital, with terrible injuries.

The Queen sent a message of sympathy, by telegram, to the families of the victims. Home Secretary Roy Jenkins arrived in Guildford under police escort the following day and he toured the scene of the explosions.

Four of the accused people subsequently spent 16 years in jail amid huge controversy (which was to become known as the "Guildford Four" case) and which developed during the intervening years.

The four men were subsequently released after judicial inquiries following the publication several years earlier of Robert Kee's book, *Trial and Error*.

**Wreckage at The Seven Stars Pub, after it was bombed on 5th October 1974.**

Discotheque equipment inside the bomb-shattered Horse and Groom.

Guildford shoppers pass the boarded-up Seven Stars pub after the blast.

Byfleet demolition firm, Ebenezer Mears and Son, pulled down the unsafe section of the Horse and Groom pub.

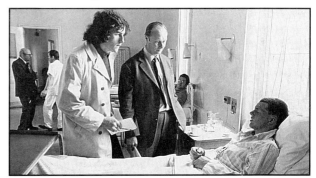

Bombing victims recovering at the Royal Surrey Hospital, Guildford.

Nearby shops were rocked by the blasts.

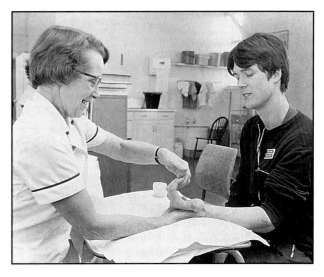

A physiotherapist working with a Guildford bombing victim, who was at the RAF rehabilitation unit at Chessington, where he was recovering from his injuries in March 1975.

# Guildford in 1975

A 23 bus on its way to Ewhurst, by way of Shamley Green and Cranleigh, stops at Guildford Bus Station on 7th January 1974. Behind it, in the course of demolition, is the Friary Meux brewery, later the site of the Friary Centre. Rationalisation in the Sixties led Ind Coope to believe that it could supply all its customers from its Romford plant in Essex. The last Ind Coope brew at Guildford was in January 1969. The site was sold to MFPC, a property development company and during late 1973 and 1974, the 1897 buildings were demolished, leaving Guildford without a brewery after many centuries, although the Hog's Back Brewery, at Tongham, just off the Hog's Back, now supplies the free trade in the area.

Much of the news in early 1975 was still dominated by the pub bombings of the previous October. As the trials of the accused began, the *Surrey Daily Advertiser* covered every aspect of the case.

Away from the courts, everyday life continued. Reports of discontent, protests and grisly events seemed to grab the headlines. The year began badly for some Guildford shopkeepers, left reeling from the destruction caused by vandals early on New Year's Day. Gangs roaming the streets after pub closing time, smashed windows at the DHSS offices in Haydon Place, at Jean Machine in Market Street, at Gregory's in Bridge Street, the Guildford Hi-Fi Centre and at Mac market.

Two Guildford people had a nice surprise at breakfast time, when they were named in the New Year Honours List. Mr Edward Louis Britton, 65, of Nightingale Road, was knighted for his services to education, having been the general secretary, vice-president and president of the National Union of Teachers. A more famous son of Guildford was also knighted. He was P.G. Wodehouse, famous creator of Bertie Wooster. Wodehouse, born in Guildford, had many of his early plays, such as *Come On, Jeeves*, first performed in the town. Aged 93, he was living in the USA when the honour was announced.

President of the Guildford Lions, Mr Bill Blake, made the headlines after a mercy trip of some 2,000 miles with clothes and supplies, to help Greek Cypriot refugees suffering from the Turkish invasion the previous year. As a reward, he got to shake hands with Archbishop Makarios.

**Guildford High Street on the damp, snowy afternoon of 27th March 1975. A Spectra van at the bottom left of the picture is promoting colour TVs.**

Multi-millionaire, Mr John Paul Getty, announced for the second year running that he would be presenting a prize of £21,000 to the person who had made the greatest contribution to the cause of wildlife conservation. One of Getty's weekend guests at Sutton Place, just outside Guildford, was a certain Captain Jacques Cousteau, who arrived to talk about sea pollution.

In February, TV personality Richard baker opened a new day room at St.Luke's Hospital. It was part of the geriatric centre and some £3,000 was raised by the Hospital's League of Friends, Rotaract and the WRVS.

The Royal family, in sombre mood, arrived at Worplesdon for a funeral service. The Queen, the Queen Mother, Princess Anne and Princess Margaret, attended St.Mary's Parish Church, Worplesdon, to pay their last respects to Reverend the Honourable Andrew Elphistone, the Queen's cousin and godfather of Princess Anne. He had assisted at her wedding to Captain Mark Phillips on 14th November 1973, at Westminster Abbey.

The Worplesdon church was packed, but the crowds outside were kept to a minimum by heavy rain and secrecy over the visit.

One important visit to Guildford did not go unnoticed however. Top pop group 10cc played at the Civic Hall in the spring and the venue's capacity of 1,040 seats were completely sold out. Somehow, more than 1,400 fans managed to get in and there were rumours of tickets being forged or re-sold at the door. Fans complained that people who had paid for tickets were left to stand and that exits were blocked.

Complaints and protests were a feature of the area and one example was the controversy at Surrey University, where students went on a rent strike, because they considered that a new weekly rent figure of £5.75 was excessive.

When the non-payers were threatened with court action by the university, they took their campaign further. Two hundred students took over the university's Senate House building and staged a one-day sit-in. Things got worse for the university authorities later on, when teaching staff decided that they would carry out strike action over a weighting allowance dispute.

Five independent transport groups urged the government to re-think its decision to pull out of the Channel Tunnel project, stating that Surrey's roads would be "murdered' by all the extra freight.

In May of 1975 the final go-ahead was given for the building of the Friary shopping centre in the town centre. The last of many objections and

**Police staged an underwater rescue demonstration in the River Wey, beneath the Guildford town centre bridge in 1975. Some shoppers believed the dummy was a real body. After all, the date was 1st April...**

appeals was quashed in a ruling from the Secretary of State for the Environment.

In April, regulars at the Spread Eagle public house started a petition to save their 'local,' which was threatened by brewery demolition. They could be seen regularly in the High Street, collecting signatures.

Another person, unhappy with brewery bosses, was Mr Noel Burch, president of the West Surrey National Union of Licensed Victuallers Association. He warned that beer prices could rise steeply in the year. This came about because the association's national body had asked for 3p to be put on the price of a pint because of an increase in rents and rates by the breweries. Mr Burch was quoted as saying: "Before the year is out you are going to have to pay 30p for a pint of bitter, there is no doubt."

Other financial advice for local people came from the Abbey National. A spokesman for that building society claimed that first-time buyers in Guildford should be earning nearly £100 a week to be able to afford a modest semi-detached house.

Death and murder were in the headlines early in the year. On 6th January a young soldier hanged himself from the railings outside the Yvonne Arnaud Theatre. A murderer died in an horrific accident on the A246 Guildford to Leatherhead road. Frederick Smith, convicted in 1947 for the 'Babes in the Wood' killings, lost control of his motor bike which ended up under a van and burst into flames. Smith was originally sentenced to death in 1947, at Kingston Assizes, for the murders of nine-year-old Leslie Gaff and his seven-year-old sister, Eileen, both of them from Southway, Guildford. He was later reprieved and spent 24 years in jail.

A Merrow man was jailed for life, at the Old Bailey, for attempted murder. The man, who hated prostitutes, planned to kill one in Soho. He had intended, for years, to strip, whip and rob the girl, then cut her throat and suck out her blood.

Mysterious killings were again in the news, later in the year, but this time concerning pets. In one night alone, 11 rabbits were slaughtered at Jacob's Well, three at Bellfields and one at Park Barn. The police were mystified.

The perpetrator broke into hutches and the rabbits were killed by blows to the head. In another incident a shed had been broken into at Park Barn and five finches and a budgerigar had been killed.

Radio One DJ, Tony Blackburn, 32, came to Guildford on 2nd October 1974, to open a new social group, the Spectrum Club, in the town. His popular breakfast show had recently been handed over to Noel Edmonds.

The new Ford Escort Ghia is launched at Gray's showrooms in Guildford on 4th March 1975.

Students stage a strike at the University of Surrey, Guildford, on 20th February 1975, as part of a demonstration against rent increases.

**Above and below: students occupying the Senate House Building at the University of Surrey, Guildford, on 3rd March 1975, during their sit-in protest over increases taking rents to £5.75 per week. Guildford Cathedral can be seen through the windows in the upper picture.**

# Godalming's a-Wombling

Godalming Primary School pupils and teachers gather for a group photograph on 5th March 1975. Note the girl at the front carrying a toy Womble.

From a Wombles 1974 record cover.

*Sit-in protest as cinema closes*

# Growing up in Godalming

When the town's Odeon Cinema closed in 1975, youngsters staged a sit-in protest, in a bid to force a re-think by the owners. The young people refused to budge from their seats when one of the last films was shown, but their demonstration proved fruitless and Godalming's Odeon was converted into a bingo hall.

The cinema closed on 14th December 1975, after 40 years. It had opened on Friday, 2nd August 1935, when it was known as The Regal, and the brochures for that big day advertised the showing of The Scarlet Pimpernel, for the launch, which was attended by the Mayor of Godalming, Alderman W.F.Paine JP.

In the Seventies, young people also found another place in which to congregate — the launderette. The Amazon washeteria, at 146, High Street, attracted people who had just left home and found mum was no longer there to do the washing.

The Richmond Arms, opposite, had a landlord, about this time, who had a racehorse trained by a vet called Underwood, who lived near Unstead, on the edge of town. One year, the horse, Harpist, won the race at Plumpton and there were celebrations in the pub.

Beer fans began to sneer at keg beers such as Watney's Red Barrel and looked for real ales instead. This move prompted the formation of the Campaign for Real Ale, in 1971, after moves by the Society for the Preservation of Beer from the Wood.

Guinness was a favourite tipple for some people in the Rose and Crown, Mill Lane, until the kegs started to be questioned by patrons.

In the '70s, traffic still flowed down the narrow High Street, making it dangerous for shoppers. Pedestrians always lived in fear of lorry wing mirrors striking them as they went about their daily

**Godalming Townswomen's Guild staged a fashion show on 30th April 1975.**

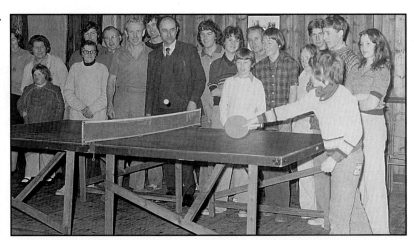

**Youngsters take part in a sponsored table tennis match at Hascombe Village Hall, near Godalming, on 22nd February 1975.**

tasks. A campaign for a bypass reached fever pitch and there was even a plan to build a road across the picturesque Lammasland Meadows, beside the river.

There were still a lot of truly local shops in the town, as late as the Seventies. The London Stores, in Church Street, was kept by a Mr Kirby who used to produce his own bacon.

At Rothwell's, the butcher's, shoppers could order their meat and then pay a woman in the cubicle.

# Shopping in Godalming, 1974

Godalming still kept much of its rural charm in the Seventies but its potential tranquillity was marred by loud traffic thundering through the town. In 1974, the High Street had the following traders:

near the junction with Bridge Street was the International Stores, selling grocery provisions. At 6, High Street, was Cardinals, the dry cleaners, T. Wong and P.J. Heather lived in the two properties next door and H. Du Bora, outfitter, was based at No.10. Jackson's, the baker's, was at No.12 and next door was Gammons of Godalming, the drapers. Glenda Gray, ladies fashions traded next door and the Impact boutique was at 18.

P.J.Luck and Co., estate agents, occupied the next site and along from the Kings Arms and Woolpack Inn, was Stage One, menswear, at 30. Dewhurst, the butcher, was at 32, Moss the chemist, at 34, Gammons the draper, at 36 and Babyland, perambulator dealers, at 38.

Paving the way to the future at 38b, was R.F.Doyle, who sold telephone answering machines. Silver's the outfitters, was in business at 40, while next door was madame Leavesley, who dealt in gowns. After the Loseley Farm Shop came Palmer's, the pianoforte dealers and then the Waitrose supermarket.

**Christmas decorations in Godalming town centre in 1979.**

**High Street, Godalming in 1975. William Douglas' sports outfitters shop is on the right, close to The Angel Hotel.**

Then, in order, were the TSB, Peter Dominic, wine merchant, Tyler's, also wine merchants, Godalming Furnishing Co., the Tea bar Café, North's shoe shop, Le Boulangerie cake shop, Barton's hi-fit store, Lotus and Delta footwear, Madame Leavesley fashion shop, Boots, W.H.Smith, Barry's hairdressers, Raymond Wood, estate agents and, across from Moss Lane, William Douglas, sports shop.

Next to The Angel was Dressmakers and then Dawson's books and greetings cards. At 96 High Street was Curry's, electrical dealers followed by Clarke's outfitters, John Gill, photographer, various solicitors, Abbey National, Freeman's the house furnishers, the Midland Bank at no.110, Kingshott electrical engineers at 114, the Nat. West bank at 116, Knickers boutique at 120 and the Hewitt, fruiterers. After Mill Lane and the post office was Health Fare health foods, Innerspace diving equipment suppliers, Bridget sports and ladies wear, Mercury dry cleaners and Hawes and Son, opticians.

The Coffee Bar café was at 142, Heathorns turf accountants at 144 and the Amazon launderette stood at 146. Fried fish was available at Lawrence's, next to the Orange Box newsagents.

On the south side of the High Street next to The Richmond Arms stood Hebard, the florists, followed by barbecue, a takeaway restaurant, Jordan's radio dealers, Westway's fisheries, the Easing Farm Dairy and Elizabeth's Restaurant. At 133 Etherington's electrical store traded and at 131 Baby Best, the baby shop, could be found. Oxfam's gift shop was at 129 and Duncan's Chemist's at 127. Hillyer's Bakeries traded at 125, and Foard ladies outfitters at 123.

Another ladies' outfitters, Country Fashions, operated at 117, while Perry and Barnes, estate agents, were in business next door. Rothwell's the butchers and The Bookshop were neighbours before Wilder's gift shop at 105. Tudor ladies hair fashions had premises at 103, while Attitudes fashion shop was at 101.

At 99 was Ye Olde Curiosity Shoppe, antiques and at 93 the premises were used by Messenger May Baverstock, chartered surveyors, estate agents and valuers. Next to them was Pitchers, Rillings and Edmonds Ltd., tailors and outfitters. Miss Mutton, the chiropodist based herself at 91a, Rainbow the tobacconist at 89 and Barclay's Bank at 87. Next to Hoar Sanderson and Spooner, estate agents, at 85, was the Wimpy Bar and a little up the street, Penny lane, ladies outfitters, Hilton's shoe shop and Hydraheat Ltd. Other stores along the same side included Fine Fare at 71, The International Tea Company at 65, Lasseter's glassware at 47, Field Brothers newsagents at 43 and Trimwell (Buttons) Ltd, tailors' sundriesmen at 29.

The open air market closed for two weeks in January 1975 amid controversy that it was doing the town's traders no good. It later re-opened.

# Jean's scene - playscheme, 1975

**From 1975, Waverley Council, whose head office is at Godalming, sponsored a number of playschemes around the borough. One was in Farnham, on the Memorial Hall site in West Street, adjacent to the Crosby Doors factory, which was demolished in the 1990s to make way for a housing and factory complex. The 1975 Farnham scheme was organized by Jean Parratt, the adult on the right of the picture, assisted by her daughter, Deborah, centre, back row, Erika Johnson, centre, and Margaret Mullery, extreme left. During the 20 days which the scheme ran, 595 different youngsters took part in Farnham, with an average attendance of five sessions, each giving an overall figure of 2,785. Many family groups can be seen above including the Wolversons, Frizzells, Roses, Van Noordens, Penns, Tuckers, Mullerys, Jones', Collins', Horsefalls and Kannemeyers.**

# Farnham girls on parade

Short dresses were in vogue when this picture was taken at the junction of South Street and Union Road, Farnham, in March 1970. It shows the entries in a personality girl contest, held at Farnham Methodist Church. The winner was Janet Knowles, of North Camp, Farnborough, (second from right). In second place was Gillian Knowles, from Rowledge (eighth from left), and third was Tina Howard of Merrow (second from left). On Gillian's left is her club-mate, Janet Hipkin, and on her right are the two Farnham entries, Nicola Cate and Helen Tissier. The winner's prize was a weekend at the Hayling Island holiday camp. A disco, run by Bob Scott, was held at the finals.

Fern Motors won an industry award on 3rd March, 1970, for the best petrol salesman. The garage at East Street, Farnham, is seen here with advertisements for tights at 4/11d - the last year of the old-style currency, before the introduction of decimalisation. Petrol was 6/2d (31p) per gallon, for two-star.

Youngsters spent the 1969-70 Christmas and New Year break converting the old East Street post office, in Farnham, into a coffee bar for the town's youth. The mural was painted by Sarah Bradpiece, who is seen standing beside it. The project was sponsored by the Rector of Farnham, Canon Donald Gray.

The coffee bar, called "Nowhere," at the former East Street post office, in Farnham, opened on Saturday 14th November 1970. It was a hectic night and all next day there was "non-stop" business, according to the *Farnham Herald*. Canon Gray, one of the major sponsors of the project, can be seen drinking a cup of coffee.

The vicar of Hale, Rev. Michael Sellors, enters into the party spirit in the "March of the Mods," one of the dances at Hale Parish party in January 1970.

Helen Tissier and Nicola Cate, two hopefuls in the Farnham Methodist Church personality girl contest pictured on 16th February 1970.

# Cranleigh, Ewhurst and Forest Green

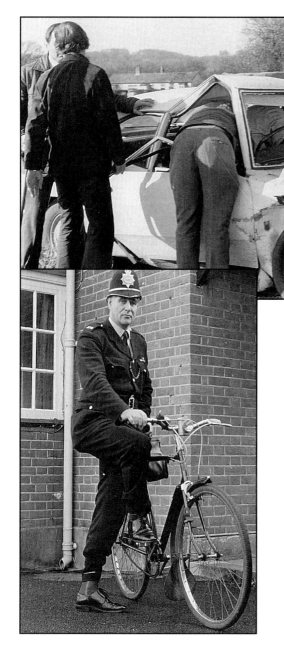

A road accident at Forest Green, near Ewhurst, on 25th April 1975.

Cranleigh's beat bobby, Pc Copus, pictured outside the village's police station in May 1975.

## Clapton's bad luck, twice in one year

Rock music legend and Ewhurst resident, Eric Clapton, had a bad start to 1975. A man described as "a close friend" was in court at Guildford, charged with the theft of goods from the guitarist's home.

These included a Gibson guitar. Worse was to come later in the year when Clapton spent three days in the Royal Surrey Hospital, Guildford, suffering from concussion.

His Ferrari and a lorry were involved in a head-on collision half-a mile from his home. Firemen from Dorking had to cut Clapton from the wreckage.

In January 1975, Cranleigh people united in a big battle to save the local village hospital from closure. They faced a lengthy fight to retain the hospital, which catered for the elderly, terminally ill and children.

Top, top right and right: pupils at Cranleigh First School in various activities in April and May 1975. Left above, Cranleigh School pupils learn how to build a car.

# Vietnamese children arrive in Haslemere and Camberley

*One hundred Vietnamese orphans arrived in Haslemere and Camberley in April 1975, from war-torn Saigon. They were on one of the last children's mercy mission planes to leave the country. The rescue was organized chiefly by the Ockenden venture. The plane landed at Heathrow Airport and was met by Foreign Office Minister David Ennals. Some of the children were ill and needed hospital treatment. Happily, some of the youngsters were awaiting adoption.*

# Arctic Haslemere, 1970

A cold spell gripped Surrey between 11th and 16th February 1970. At Haslemere, snow on February 12th lay thickly and disrupted traffic. Here police discuss the problems with a lorry driver in Haslemere High Street. The driver found he could not get a grip on the icy roads.

## Fleetwood Mac's home at Hindhead

Members of Fleetwood Mac, one of the Seventies' most successful rock bands, whose album, Rumours, (1977) has sold more than 25 million copies, worldwide, lived at Hindhead in the Seventies. It was: "A large, white house with lovely big open spaces, where we all used to play hide and seek," according to farmer's son, Zac Miller, who visited the mansion as a child with his mother, a friend of the band's Mick Fleetwood. "I remember running away from this giant of a man with a beard."

Haslemere 18 plus club held a vicars and tarts party on 11th March 1970.

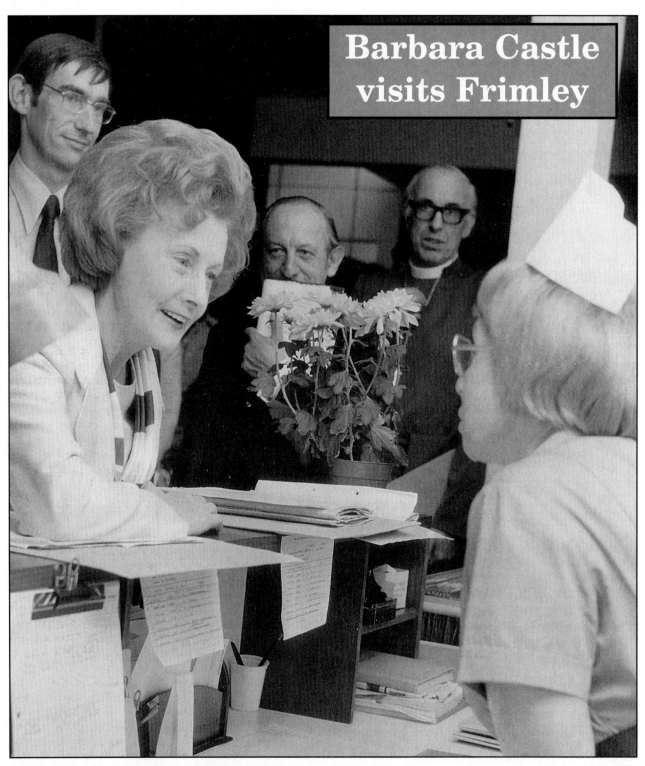

**Barbara Castle visits Frimley**

**Mrs Barbara Castle, then Social Services Secretary, opened the new Frimley Park Hospital, Frimley, on 30th April, 1975, despite a protest from 200 members of the local branch of the National Federation for the Self-employed.**

**Dorking High Street in the Seventies. On the left is W.H.Smith, Halfords, Peter Lord and farther down the road, Tesco, which was to close in January 1986 and then be demolished to make way for the St. Martin's Walk shopping centre, next to Mill Lane. Originally Tesco was only a food shop but it later expanded its range and "went into everything," recalled a Dorking pensioner.**

## *'Spirit of Uri Geller bent Brockham couple's cutlery'*

# Dorking in early 1974

During the first week of January 1974, the doors finally closed on Dorking's Cellar Club, in South Street, amid a storm of protest.

For five years, the club at the former Methodist Church buildings had been regularly attended, six nights a week, by anything from 100 to 150 of the town's teenagers.

Angry youngsters launched a major battle to save the club and wrote to Dorking's MP, Sir George Sinclair, and planned a protest march.

Windows at the church were smashed and angry notices stuck high up on walls. Reverend Donald Rawlings, minister of the Dorking Methodist Church, said he sympathised with the teenagers and had promised them they could stay until the bulldozers arrived. Club member, Bernard Fishlock, told the *Dorking Advertiser*: "The youth of Dorking have no cinemas, no disco

clubs; only pubs are left for us in this town. What clubs do the council run for youngsters who want to listen to their kind of music six nights a week?"

Meanwhile, another protest was taking place over the move to Meadowbank, Dorking, by the Guildford City F. C., in a merger with Dorking F.C. The clubs' supporters were against the merger, but shareholders voted in favour of the relocation. Some of the city players signed an 806-name petition against the move from Guildford's Bannisters Farm ground. They lost their battle. However, about three years later, the merged clubs again hit financial troubles and folded. Dorking emerged from the ashes and rose again.

Conductor and composer, André Previn, who lived at Bunce Common Road, Leigh, denied a story that he had applied for British citizenship.

From Monday, 7th January, all second deliveries of post to rural areas around Dorking, were

**The Wheatsheaf in Dorking High Street some years before the last pints were pulled there on 20th January, 1974. The pub was restored and later became a bookshop called Book Ends.**

suspended, owing to the fuel crisis.

A Brockham couple, after watching psychic metal-twister, Uri Geller, on TV, had to summon the vicar in the middle of the night, to drive out a spirit which, they said, was terrorising them and bending their cutlery and jewellery. Later, a Westcott churchman warned of the dangers of dabbling with the occult and Uri Geller's fork-bending activities. Pastor Jim Allis, of St. John's Free Church, Westcott, said people were putting themselves in terrible danger.

In January, too, plans were afoot to open Dorking Museum, in West Street. The Department of the Environment turned down a scheme to build a housing estate which would have doubled the size of Beare Green. In 1974, a bright, modern semi-detached house in Dorking would have cost in the region of £13,950. An end-of-terrace, three-bedroom home was advertised for £16,500. By late January, The Wheatsheaf pub in Dorking High Street, had closed down.

The *Dorking Advertiser* reported: "There must have been 120 people in the bars at any one time on the last day. Publican, Norman Merrick, sat on the other side of the bar for a change and was served by friends and volunteers who acted as barmen for the evening.

"The drinks flowed fast and furiously and by the end of the evening only a few bottles of cider and a couple of bottles of Mackeson remained."

Mr. Merrick and his wife became postmasters of Mickleham post office. It was reported that The Wheatsheaf was haunted by a "benevolent" ghost.

Other topics of the day also made headlines. Despite an acute police shortage, crime in Dorking fell by 20 per cent in 1973-4, Chief Constable Peter Mathews reported. The Government's spending axe fell on a plan to build an £87,000 Dorking First School, at Ranmore Road, for 160 children.

A farm worker, aged 22, died after falling off a haystack at the Coldharbour home of film star, Oliver Reed, on 18th January.

After a two-year fight, campaigners claimed a victory when plans to put up electricity pylons, between Leigh and Dorking, were dropped. Angry caravan owners at Box Hill rejected proposals to run down the mobile home site, at a meeting in the Hand-in-Hand Hall, next door to the public house of the same name.

Massive cuts in government spending threw plans for comprehensive education, in Dorking, into chaos. Gales and floods also caused mayhem in the district on 10th February. One large pine crashed through the roof of a house in The Glebe, Dorking.

Dorking Hospital Radio planned to launch its first programme in February.

The Embassy Cinema closed in 1973, leaving the town with no cinema screens. This 1,200-seat cinema, designed by Harry Weston, opened in 1938, as the Gaumont. It stood where, in modern times, Mole Valley Council's Pippbrook car park was constructed, opposite the Dorking Halls. The Embassy building was used by Jehovah's Witnesses until it was demolished in 1983.

All the latest sounds were available in 1974, at Track and Groove Record Shop in Dorking High Street.

The Romano Coffee House stands derelict in North Street, Dorking, in the mid 1970s. The previous decade, the premises were the Tirola Café, a favourite haunt of Dorking's youth. On the window, "Bill Stickers," has pasted up a poster advertising a concert at Guildford's Civic Hall, by Gong, described by pop historians as a "hippie-based surreal" group whose members once included guitarist Steve Hillage.

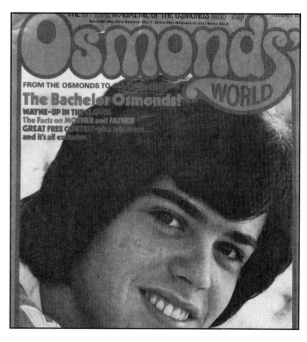

Teenage heart-throb, Donny Osmond, whose hit records, such as "Puppy Love," could be bought at Dorking's Track and Groove record store, in 1972.

Dorking Motor Company advertises its new models, early in 1974.

A new-style stereo system is promoted in 1974, by S.J.Clear's shop in Dorking High Street.

# Dorking boy on TV's Police 5

## *Re-enactment of murder in bid for clues*

Philip Doyle, aged 13, the son of Dorking's CID chief, was seen by millions of TV viewers in November 1970, when he appeared in a murder reconstruction on Police Five.

He re-enacted the last movements of 14-year-old Brockham schoolboy, Roy Tutill, who was found strangled on the Beaverbrook estate near Mickleham, early on 26th April, 1968.

Police stated, on Shaw Taylor's TV show, that grease marks found on the boy's shirt, revealed a pattern found in the boots of many cars, particularly Vauxhalls.

Another clue was that a thread, found lying across Roy's face, was from upholstery or curtain material, of a cotton/rayon mixture.

The boy's killer was never brought to justice and may now be dead, police believe.

Inspector Doyle later retired to Ireland.

TV viewers aid murder hunt

CALLERS blocked a police switchboard yesterday after a TV reconstruction of a murder.

More than 80 people phoned police at Dorking, Surrey, to offer help in the search for the killer of 14-year-old Roy Tutill, who was found strangled in a wood two-and-a-half years ago.

Philip Doyle, 13, son of Dorking's CID chief, played the part of the dead boy in a recon-struction of his last hours on London Weekend's *Police Five*.

Detective Chief Inspector Philip Doyle also showed viewers three clues which had not been made public before :

1. A thread found lying across Roy's face. Tests showed that it came from upholstery or curtain material of a cotton rayon mixture.

2. Grease marks on the boy's shirt in a pattern found in the boots of many cars, particularly Vauxhalls.

3. A photograph taken the day Roy was found. It showed a group of people in the garden of a public house near where his body was dumped. Police want to trace a man and a girl in the picture.

Humble beginnings: in the early 1970s, there was just a caravan snack bar at the Burford Bridge car park at the foot of Box Hill. By the late Seventies and early Eighties, hundreds of bikers arrived on Sundays to patronize the recently-expanded kiosk, by now called Rykas.

Dorking DJ, Dave Shiers, has been a familiar sight in the town's pubs since 1971, when he started spinning the discs at the Star and Garter, near Dorking Station, as a teenager. He was later a frequently seen face in Murray's Wine Bar, Dorking High Street. This venue started in 1979, when it was owned by a Mr Murray as a respectable wine bar. Formerly it was the Spanish Olé Restaurant. Mr Murray soon sold the business and Keith Giles, a bar manager, started running it. DJ Shiers is pictured here, with his discotheque, at Beare Green Village Hall, in about 1978.

DJ Dave Shiers, pictured in about 1979, at Chart Downs Estate, Dorking.

One of 10cc's best-known albums, Deceptive Bends, was named after the hazard sign on the A24 at Mickleham, near Dorking. This album cover has been signed by the band and presented to Dorking builder, Fred Coombe. It reads: "Best Wishes to Fred, the man himself!"

## *10cc, Abba and Cliff Richard used Strawberry Studios*

# Rock stars in Dorking

The 1970s were synonymous with the sounds of the melodic rock group 10cc. In the hot summer of 1975, discos would often end with I'm Not In Love - the band's most successful single, and radio stations, even today, still frequently play Rubber Bullets, Dreadlock Holiday and Good Morning, Judge.

In 1976, 10cc forged an important link with Dorking, when they bought the Strawberry Studios, in South Street. The former Pavilion Cinema, which closed in September 1963, was converted into one of the world's top studios, by Dorking builder, Fred Coombe , to a design by Tom Hindley.

In the following five years, 10cc, Cliff Richard, Sad Café and occasionally, Abba, used the studios. 10cc recorded their Deceptive Bends album there in early 1977. It was named after the road sign bearing the same words, which used to stand at the Mickleham bends, on the A24.

The band recorded follow-up albums, Bloody Tourists and 10cc - Ten Out Of Ten, plus the 45rpm singles, The Things We Do For Love, Good Morning Judge and Dreadlock Holiday at Dorking's Strawberry South studios.

The silent, fully air-conditioned studios were impressive, futuristic and spacious. As well as offering the most advanced equipment, they also provided a homely atmosphere with warm colours and thick carpets.

"There was room for a 70-piece orchestra," Fred Coombe recalled many years later. "The studio was very complex because of the type of insulation used. There were floating floors, velvet curtains, walls covered with Portuguese oak and hundreds upon hundreds of sound baffles, which

**Inside part of the soundproofed Strawberry Studios at Dorking.**

would be hidden away.

"Everything was variable, with hard or soft surfaces, mirrors and louvred walls."

The control room, studio, mirror-walled isolation room, conference room and workshop were on the ground floor and upstairs was a bathroom, kitchen, dining room, 'snackery,' and 'snuggery' - a modern, circular room with seats all the way round for sitting, reading and watching TV. There was also Graham Gouldman's small bedroom which he used when the work schedule was heavy and he could not get home.

Tom Hindley, the designer of the four-storey studios, was a colourful character, with long hair and '70s-style fashionable clothes. He would sometimes arrive in South Street by helicopter. On entering the premises through the back door, an assistant would announce, repeatedly: "Make way for Tom Hindley."

Hindley lived in Switzerland and his home apparently overlooked Lake Lucerne. Near the front entrance to the studio was a large painting of

a maid, holding a feather duster and bending down.

Eric Stewart, from 10cc, at that time lived in a large house called Colombe, off the Dorking Road, near Walton-on-the-Hill. The roof was undulating and seemed to be shaped just like the switchback Dorking Road. During his time in Surrey, Eric Stewart was involved in a terrible car accident on the A25 Reigate Road, near Buckland, and suffered serious injuries. On leaving the area he moved to an Elizabethan mansion in Kent.

**The front cover of the studio's brochure.**

**The mirrored walls in a section of the luxurious studio.**

Redhill High Street on 26th November 1975. On the far left is the Market Hall, which dated back to 1860 and was pulled down in 1982. On the corner of the High Street and Station Road was Burton's gents' clothes shop. Next to it was a branch of the Woolwich Building Society, then Ripolin, a stockist of wallpaper and home decorating items.

Station Road, Redhill, on 26th November 1975. A slogan in the Wimpy Bar window reads: "Is your yummy tumbling?" Partners leather goods shop is on the right, opposite Forte's Café, where many a weary shopper would relax, enjoying a cheap roast dinner or a Welsh rarebit snack, under the metallic revolving fans.

**Redhill housewives and pensioners queuing for bread on 6th November 1978, at The Pantry, Station Road, Redhill, during the shortage owing to strike action by Bakers Union members.The previous September also saw similar scenes and at Acres the Bakers, Redhill.**

*Queues for bread as union calls a strike*

# Shopping in Redhill, 1978

Food shopping in Redhill in the late Seventies was carried out chiefly at Sainsbury's, the Co-op, Tesco and the relatively new Safeway supermarket.

Tesco was opposite Jenning's stationery and toy shop in the High Street, but it was soon to close.

The Co-op, at the other end of town, near the post office, was to survive for a few more years. One of its attractions was a small cafeteria, where staff would prepare filled rolls to order. The Fine Fare supermarket in the centre of the High Street had long since disappeared.

At Sainsbury's, in November 1978, half a dozen eggs cost 19p; half-a-pound of butter cost 29½ p, a quarter pound of tea was 14½ p and a 15oz can of baked beans cost 12p. Sainsbury's was trading in Station Road, close to the junction with St. Matthews Road in the Seventies, having relocated many years earlier from premises at the lower end of Station Road, near Rhythms music shop. Two toilet rolls cost 19½p and half a pound of back bacon cost 64p.

Shoppers had enormous problems obtaining bread during November 1978, owing to a strike by Bakers Union members.

The *Surrey Mirror* reported that "Housewives in the borough were forced to join a frantic hunt-the-loaf scramble, as bread supplies in the shops were sliced by more than half." To add to the misery, there were train strikes and industrial action was threatened by nurses at the Royal Earlswood Hospital.

Queues stretched along the street from The Pantry baker's in Station Road, opposite Safeway, and at one stage nearly 30 men and women waited in the hope of getting a loaf.

Local bakers, such as Anthony Jackson, in Holmesdale Road, Reigate, trebled their production, but supplies were sold out by mid-morning. The Pantry, in Reigate High Street, reported queues forming outside at eight a.m., when they did not open until nine a.m. All these difficulties were to be exacerbated in the winter of 1978-79, as more and more unions called strikes.

It was to become known as the Winter of Discontent and proved to be a great strain on the Prime Minister, James Callaghan, who was to remain in power for only a few more months, after which Margaret Thatcher replaced him on 4th May 1979.

Traffic still flowed southwards when this picture was taken on 26th November 1975. On the left is The Towers public house, which offered musical entertainment for young people in the late Seventies. Its name was later changed to Crocks but in the 1990s it re-emerged as The Office. The Tower wine stores attached to the Courage premises vanished with the name of Towers. Farther down the High Street is a 447 single-decker bus, picking up passengers on its circuitous route.

The car park behind the Victorian shops and flats in Station Road, Redhill, opposite The Arcade, which were demolished to make way for McDonalds and the Warwick Quadrant, in the 1980s. The derelict babywear shop over the road has posters in the window advertising a concert by Seventies rock band Slade.This picture was taken on 6th April 1978.

Going, going, gone... The Victorian parade in Station Road, Redhill, which contained The South Eastern public house, is pulled down. Opposite is The Arcade, which survived the bulldozer's onslaught. This picture was taken on 6th April 1978. In 1975, The South Eastern's manager was James Hanley, whose brother, Don, was landlord of the Caterham Arms pub in Caterham, which was bombed by terrorists on 27th August 1975.

# The end of an era at a Redhill public house

**Sybil Star, outside the Home Cottage, Redhill, on 27th September 1978. She had run the pub since 1939.**

A chapter in Redhill's history closed on 29th June 1975, when the town's best-known pub landlady pulled her last pint after 40 years behind the bar.

Sybil Star had run the Home Cottage on Redstone Hill, Redhill, since 1939 but the pub had been in her family's name since 1887. In her time at the Home Cottage, the public house had become a popular haunt of real ale fans.

It was Miss Star's grandmother who first bought the Home Cottage and it was here that Sybil was born in 1901. She was brought up at the pub, with her sister and two brothers, while her mother, Jane, ran the establishment. The premises had remained virtually unaltered in the four decades Sybil had been in charge. She said at the time: "It would take heavy financial involvement to change it."

Incredibly, Sybil took no holiday leave at all. The only break she had in all that time was a trip to Canada in 1951. She told the *Surrey Mirror*

that, apart from that, she had not had a single day off. Remarkably, Sybil rarely had anything to drink. She said at the time: "I never drink. I only have the occasional sherry if I visit my brother. It is the beginning of the end if you have a pub and drink."

And of her hard work, she said: "My philosophy is to get on with a job and not grumble about it. The thing is to stick at it and not let anything put you off."

Local people recall that she did not approve of smoking and anyone asking at the bar for cigarettes was looked at somewhat disapprovingly. She also prohibited couples from holding hands on the premises. Young's Brewery took over upon her retirement. Sybil, who was 77 at the time of her retirement, liked Redhill and decided to live locally, with friends.

She died in the following decade, but she is still remembered by hundreds of her patrons over the years.

The Odeon, Redhill, pictured on 24th September 1975, the week in which its impending closure the following month was announced. Showing at the time was Shampoo (X), starring Warren Beatty, Julie Christie and Goldie Hawn.

*No tears, just a few moist eyes as cinema closes*

# Closure of The Odeon, Redhill

Redhill's Odeon Cinema closed for good on Saturday 18th October 1975. The last film to be shown was "That Lucky Touch," but nobody cried on the last night. According to eye-witnesses, only a few film-goers had moist eyes and as they left the building they muttered a few words of condolence to the cimena staff who had lost their jobs.

It was a sad time for manager Ted Moss. He had tried many publicity stunts over the years in a bid to draw in the crowds.He played the violin on the cinema's roof for "Fiddler on the Roof," got hold of a Volkswagen car for "Herbie Rides Again" and in the summer of 1975, he found someone to dress up as a swordsman for "The Four Musketeers." He did not turn up on the last night because the occasion would have been too painful for him, he told reporters.

The cinema was opened in 1938, the year that they started making "Gone With the Wind" in Hollywood. Rank claimed that by 1974 it was uneconomical, losing £10,000 in a year.

In its final week, only a trickle of people turned up and there was certainly no funeral atmosphere among the 200 folk who attended the final night, the *Surrey Mirror* reported. Earlier in the week, a farewell party had been held by the staff, who included assistant manager Betty Jardine.They brought out an iced cake and presented it to Ted Moss, for his outstanding dedication to the cinema, which was owned by Rank.

After major internal refurbishment, the Odeon building, which stands opposite Redhill station, re-opened as Busby's discotheque and nightclub. A few years later, the club's name was changed to The Millionaire. Redhill also mourned the loss of another facility a few years earlier — the swimming baths, off the London Road.

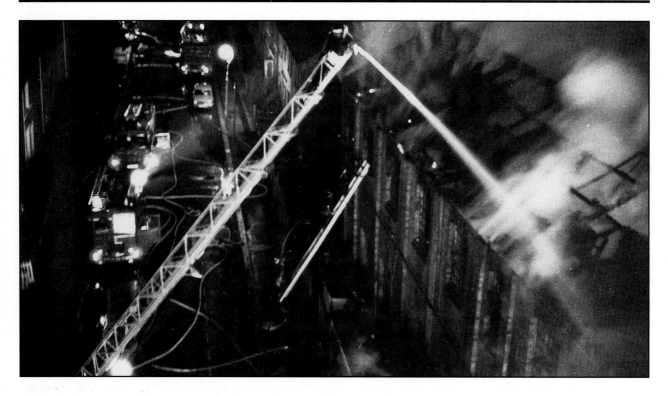

**Fire swept through the former Kennings Garage in Cecil Road, Redhill, on the night of 8th January 1975. Reigate and Banstead Council was in the process of buying the Victorian properties at the time, to make way for the redevelopment of Redhill town centre.**

**Firemen tackle a major fire in an annexe of the St. Anne's Nursing Home, Redhill, on 7th April 1975. Fifty firemen were called to the blaze, which made two families homeless. The Victorian buildings which once stood prominently on the Redhill skyline, were demolished soon after and the site was cleared in preparation for the Noke Drive housing estate.**

Redhill's Market Hall survived until the end of the Seventies, but in 1982, it was demolished to make way for a new development. This photograph was taken just after the 1979 Christmas holiday period. Seven years later, HRH the Duke of Gloucester opened the new Warwick Quadrant shopping centre and Harlequin Theatre, built on the site of the Market Hall. Its loss is still mourned by many townsfolk, some of whom enjoyed browsing around the bric-a-brac stalls in the building on Saturdays in the late Seventies. Among other uses, the small rooms on the ground floor were hired by the *Surrey Mirror*, so that shorthand lessons could be given by dedicated tutor, Mrs Joan Stritch, who lived for many years in Westway Gardens, Redhill. Outside the building stood the bus information kiosk. The Market Hall was built in 1860.

A general view of Redhill market, which opened on 7th September 1978. There had been a long campaign for an open market in the town and eventually a site between Cecil Road and Ladbroke Road was selected. The ribbon was cut by Irish comedian Frank Carson, assisted by the deputy mayor, councillor Frank Hutchinson, who braved the rain to conduct the ceremony.

**The driver of this E-reg. Ford Cortina came to grief in Gatton Bottom, Merstham, in the snowy conditions of March 1975.**

*Unseasonal snow in 1975*

# Shivering at Easter

Easter 1975 got off to a snowy start in Surrey, but this was not the last of the unseasonal weather. On 2nd June 1975, snow started to fall over the downland areas and children at de Stafford School, Caterham, were urged by their geography teacher to go to the window and observe "something they may never see again in their lifetime." Outside, thick flakes were falling on the school's field at Burntwood Lane.

This was one of the latest times in the year snow had fallen in the 20th century. It did not settle, but with the temperature at just 35F (2C) in Caterham, it nearly did. A week later, the county was basking in a heatwave, which continued for a large part of the summer. The earlier Easter snow did not last but it did cause difficult driving conditions. Surrey County Council's gritting team, based at Weatherhill, Smallfield, kept the new M23 clear and motorway patrol leader, Chief Inspector Ray Searle,was pleased that the thin holiday traffic was kept moving.

On Thursday 27th March, the day preceding Good Friday, there were several accidents in the icy conditions. A car hit a tree in Somerset Road, Meadvale, near Redhill, injuring young Gary Dixon and his mother, Gwendoline. Three more people were hurt when their vehicle went out of control in Norman's Road, Outwood and an invalid carriage disintegrated when it skidded across the A23 at Merstham. The driver miraculously escaped serious injury.

A scuffle broke out at Reigate Hill when youths started to throw snowballs at passing motorists. Police were called to cool the situation. Surrey's farmers complained that grass was unable to grow in the cold snap and Nutfield farmer, John Shinner, feared for his raspberries.

Those wishing to escape the gloom booked tickets to see Paper Lace, Sacha Distel, The Sensational Alex Harvey Band and the Detroit Spinners, who were all giving concerts at Fairfield Halls, Croydon, in April and May 1975.

Those people buying new cars could have selected an Opel Kadett C, available from Traffic, a dealer at Walton Street, Walton on the Hill, for £1,255.

The car offered 2-star economy and "stylish looks."

The still unfinished M25 near Reigate Hill was used as an aircraft runway by Redhill farmers, in a desperate bid to beat the wet weather, in April 1975. Spring rains left the fields water-logged and impossible for tractors to work on the boggy land, but the all-important job of spreading fertiliser had to go on. To overcome the problems, Redhill farmers clubbed together to hire a plane that could zoom low of the farmland, spraying the fertiliser. With Redhill Aerodrome also too muddy, it was decided to use the M25. The motorway between Reigate and Merstham was not open to traffic until February 1976. This section had taken four years to build.

The Locomotive pub, in Ladbroke Road, Redhill. Run by Charrington's, it was still serving pints when this photograph was taken during the 1979 Christmas holiday period. It was soon demolished for redevelopment of the Princess Way bypass around the town centre.

# Sir Geoffrey lends his support

### *Huge petition for a new Redhill Hospital*

Almost 20,000 people in the East Surrey area put their names to a petition calling for a new all-purpose hospital, which could replace the outmoded Redhill General facilities at Earlswood Common.

Sir Geoffrey Howe and George Gardiner, MPs, plus newsagents and thousands of householders right across the area, signed numerous petitions in the mid-Seventies.

In the autumn of 1975, campaigners led by the *Surrey Mirror*'s Kimble Earl, took the petitions to Whitehall and demanded that health chief Barbara Castle take action.

Eventually, the petitioners succeeded in their campaign and the new East Surrey Hospital opened at South Earlswood in the early 1980s, the formal ceremony being attended by Prime Minister Mrs Margaret Thatcher.

Right: Sir Geoffrey, MP for East Surrey, joins a constituent to sign a petition calling for the new hospital to be built in the Redhill area. The picture was taken in 1975.

Left: George Gardiner, MP for Reigate, also lent his support for the new hospital campaign in 1975. Right: newsagents across East Surrey placed petitions on their counters to help the campaign. This picture was taken on 4th August 1975. The *Evening News* headline wishes the Queen Mother a happy 75th birthday with the words: "Happy Birthday, Ma'am, love from everybody." *The Sun* promises a parade of fashion girls on inside pages with the topical title 'Tubular Belles,' playing on the name of Mike Oldfield's 1974 top-selling album, whose title was spelled a little differently.

**Wintry weather causes a traffic snarl-up in Redhill High Street on 13th January 1977, delaying the 405 bus to Horley and Crawley.**

An RF 425 bus on its way from Guildford to Redhill, passes through flood water at Flanchford, between Reigate and Leigh, on 6th September 1974.

London Road, Reigate, on 18th December 1979. The Wadham Stringer garage is on the right, offering two-star petrol for £1.16 per gallon or £1.18 for four star. The garage was demolished a few years later on, after which Watson House was constructed.

# Reigate at Christmas 1974

Church Street, Reigate, takes on a glittering look for Christmas 1974. The photograph was taken on Thursday 19th December, that year, at 5.20pm. The one-way system around the town had not long been introduced and the chaos resulting from the day of the changeover had long since been forgotten. Among the shops on the right are Andrew Glass stationers; Baldwins of Reigate, chemist's and photography dealers; Robertson's high class grocery and coffee store (which closed in August 1995) and, on the corner of Tunnel Road, Tesco's, which became Muswell's café in later years. On the left is a 410 double-decker London and Country bus whose driver is taking a break before returning to Oxted, Westerham and Bromley.

Bell Street, Reigate, on 18th December, 1979, some 14 years before Safeway opened on a site to the left. On the right is the Ancient House bookshop and Stoneman's funeral services.

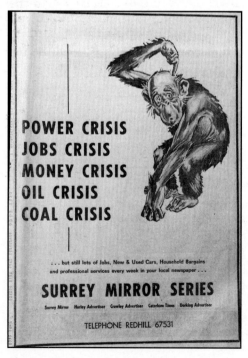

A sign of the times from the *Surrey Mirror*, early in 1974.

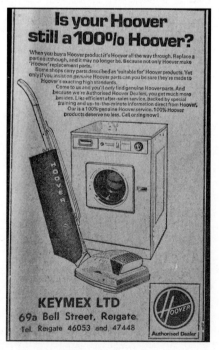

An advertisement for Hoover products which were available from Keymex, Bell Street, Reigate, in 1974.

## *Reorganization of local government*

# Horley's 1972 protest

Protestors block the road in a demonstration, during 1972, over plans to move Horley into the borough of Crawley, West Sussex. On 1st April, 1974, a huge shake-up of local government occurred in Surrey, with many of the old boroughs vanishing. Reigate, Banstead and Horley merged in the reorganization. New districts, or boroughs, such as Spelthorne, Surrey Heath, Waverley, Mole Valley and Tandridge emerged, in the biggest shake-up since 1965.

Evelyn's Café traded in the 'Wooden Hut,' which formed part of the Foresters public house in Victoria Road, Horley.

Janet Rosslyn's baby linen and schoolwear store, Chisholm's the tailor's and Bunkell's shops, Horley town centre, in August 1979.

**Horley's only cinema, The Regent, was to close soon after this picture was taken on 17th August 1979. By 1982, the building had been demolished. Martin's newsagent, and other shops, later stood on the site in Victoria Road, near its junction with Consort Way.**

*In the news, during 1974, were Prime Ministers Edward Heath, Harold Wilson and Liberal candidate, Jeremy Thorpe, whose mother, Ursula, lived at Greystones, Limpsfield. Princess Anne and Captain Mark Phillips married at Westminster Abbey on 14th November, 1973, and spent their honeymoon at White Lodge, Richmond Park.*

# Decimalisation, 15th February 1971

Decimal currency became official tender on 15th february 1971 - dubbed "D" Day, by the daily newspapers of the time.

Pennies, threepenny pieces, sixpences, shillings, florins, half-crowns and halfpennies were phased out when Britain's old coinage system, based on twelves instead of tens, was discontinued.

Shopkeepers were accused of unnecessary price rises when the change was made.

Sixpenny coins continued as 2½p tokens for several more years until they, too, were called in by the banks.

Two shilling pieces (florins), became 10 pence pieces (the large size), and shilling coins became 5 pence pieces which were then much larger than later coins of the same denomination.

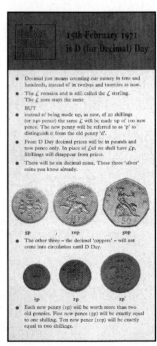

**Shoppers were given leaflets to explain the change to decimal coins.**

Sir Geoffrey Howe, MP for East Surrey, joined local Conservatives for a sponsored walk along the M25 motorway, near Godstone, which had just been completed but was within five weeks of being open to traffic, when this picture was taken on 6th October 1979.

## *Protests and praise for new motorway*

# Building of the M25

The M25 was Surrey's biggest development in the 1970s. Designed to relieve the terrible congestion in the county's towns and also London, the orbital route around the capital really got under way during this decade.

● In **September 1976**, work started on a five-mile section of the motorway, between Westerham and Godstone. The constructor was Bovis, the engineers were the South East Road Construction Unit and the scheme cost £8.4m. It was opened in November 1979.

● In **March 1972**, work began on a ten-mile section between Godstone and Reigate. The construction included a four-level, free-flow interchange at Merstham, linking up with the M23, which flies over the M25 at the highest level, on five 180ft spans. The work was carried out by French and completed in **February 1976**. The engineers were the South East Road Construction Unit and the cost was £10.4m.

● The Reigate to Leatherhead section was started in May 1983 and finished in October 1985. Originally it had been hoped to build this section before 1980.

● Leatherhead to Wisley's section saw work commence in November 1982 and by October 1985 it had been completed.

● Wisley to Chertsey's six-mile stretch was started in September 1981 and finished in December 1983.

● Chertsey to Thorpe's two-mile link was built between **July 1978** and October 1980 by Bovis at a cost of £7.6m. A main feature of the scheme was a two-span skew suspension bridge, designed by British Rail, which carries a railway over the M25. Its towers rise 100ft above the carriageway. This section also includes a multi-level, free-flow interchange with the M3.

● The Thorpe to Egham section of two miles in length, was built between **August 1974** and **December 1976** at a cost of £9.9m. Two hot, dry summers in 1975 and 1976, prevented mud problems. Here Bovis and Fairclough had to construct

**The Minister of Transport, Norman Fowler, meets protestors at the ceremony to open a new, nine-mile stretch of the M25 motorway between Godstone and Sevenoaks. At the event, on Wednesday 14th November 1979, campaigners against the new road arrived from Ashtead. But one Oxted villager said: "It's going to be like moving from Central London to Cornwall." A spokesman for Oxted Parish Council described the protestors as "empty-headed."**

an embankment 25ft high so the highway could cross the River Thames. An earth mound was formed to protect Thorpe village from noise.

● At a cost of £8.1m, the one-mile stretch between Egham and Yeoveney, forming Junction 13, connecting with the A30, was constructed between **July 1977** and November 1981. The main feature here was the building of Runnymede Bridge, some 430 feet long, which was designed to be sympathetic to the existing Lutyens bridge, built circa 1960.

# In orbit around the capital

Cutting the tape at the opening of the new M25 section between Godstone and Sevenoaks, is Mr Norman Fowler, Minister of Transport. After speeches at the ceremony, on 14th November 1979, the managing director of Gleeson Civil Engineering, Mr G. Zeronian, then handed over the motorway to Mr Fowler on behalf of his company. Mr Fowler said that the M25 was a major breakthrough for transport in Britain and was one of the first steps towards a better and more progressive transport policy. However, wear and tear on the surface of the motorway has meant that, like the Forth Bridge, work never finishes on the facility. Repair and widening work along several stretches of its length has been continuing into the Nineties.

The Café Rembahn and Henry's Snack Bar, provided snacks for travellers coming out of Oxted Station, in November 1975. These two eating places were in a building once kept as corn stores by Berry and Sons many years earlier.

Station Road West, Oxted, on 26th November 1975. Mr Butcher, the baker, is on the right, next to Ye Olde Wine Shoppe, where cigarettes were on special offer, with 1½p a packet off.

The Hoskins Hotel in Station Road West, Oxted, on 26th November 1975. Twenty years later, the hotel stood empty and burnt-out awaiting redevelopment after a fire two years earlier. The Plaza Cinema is farther up the road, on the left, and at the top of the street is the station.

*Six-course festive lunch at The Hoskins for £8.50*

# Christmas in Oxted, 1975

In the lead-up to Christmas 1975, Oxted's shopkeepers were keen to advertise their services and wares.

The Hoskins Hotel in Station Road West prepared to open on Christmas Day, offering a special six-course lunch for £8.50 and presents from Santa Claus for the children.

Barons of Oxted, in Station Road West, was also open on Christmas Day, for a traditional luncheon at £7.50 (plus service).

For 'a present of quality,' A. French Ltd at 54-62 Station Road East, offered a large range of shirts, trousers, handkerchiefs, dressing gowns and pyjamas.

Warburton Sports at Station Road West, boasted the largest selection of model kits in the area, selling Tamiya, Airfix, Revell and Matchbox.

Derrick and Joan, at the Mechanised Garden Centre, 21 Hoskins Road, suggested it was the time of the year to get the mower fixed while vacuum cleaners, such as the Hoover junior, could be purchased for £19.50 from Crown Electrical at 89 Station Road East. The store also offered a part exchange service.

Oxted Linen Company at 10 Station Road West, lured shoppers with 'the widest selection of household linens in the area' which included Dorma, Christy, Moderna, Lament and bedspreads of all types including simulated fur.

The Co-op in Oxted was charging 14½p for a large white sliced loaf; 20½p for half-a-dozen eggs, 23p for 2lbs of sugar; 35p for 5lbs of potatoes and 11½p for a 15oz tin of baked beans.

At the Plaza cinema, Oxted, some rather saucy films were being shown. On Sunday 9th November 1975, Helen Christie and Barbara Wise appeared in Escort Girls (X). Also on the double bill programme was Some Like It Sexy (X). During the following week, the cinema showed Ryan O'Neal in Love Story.

**Shoppers in Station Road East, Oxted, begin to prepare for Christmas 1975. This photograph was taken on 26th November. Christmas Day in Oxted, that year, was dull, damp and mild.**

**Woolworth's, Carter's, Decor and Lovell's were among the shops along Station Road East, Oxted, in November 1975.**

The fear of terrorism came to Redhill on 17th September 1973, when there was a bomb scare at Redhill Station. A fleet of K-reg. Escort police cars arrived at the scene and after a search, officers gave the all-clear and people were able to carry on their everyday business.

*Thirty-one injured in terrorist attack*

# Caterham pub bombing 1975

**Crowds gather outside the Caterham Arms pub shortly after the explosion on 27th August 1975**

Terrorists left a trail of devastation and horrifying injuries behind them after bombing a Caterham public house in August 1975.

A huge explosion rocked the Caterham Arms in Coulsdon Road on Wednesday 27th August, while the pub was packed with young people enjoying a discotheque.

Thirty-one people were badly injured in the blast, which tore the limbs off several soldiers from the nearby Caterham Barracks. The disco was often attended by members of the 1st Battalion Welsh Guards.

It was just after playing a Led Zeppelin song that the tremendous explosion occurred. Disc jockey Martin Ellenden, from the Deadly Nightshade Disco, Sutton, had just cleared the dance floor when the explosion ripped through the pub. He escaped injury. The wall behind his turntables was bowed by the force of the blast. Many of those present were deafened for days by the noise.

Teenage girls clambered over limb-less soldiers and barmaid Kitty Stone said at the time that there was glass everywhere and nobody could see for the smoke. Guardsman, Paul Thomas, lost both legs and an arm.

Fleets of ambulances took the injured to Redhill General Hospital as a posse of police converged on the town, sealing off roads and helping ambulancemen and fire crews to sift through the debris.

Many suffered minor injuries. Among these were Caterham girls Patricia King, Angela Scott and Angela Cole. The district's MP, Sir Geoffrey Howe, later toured the wards of Redhill General Hospital, visiting casualties and in early September, Prince Charles piloted his own red helicopter into the hospital grounds and visited the victims.

In just a week, the public had collected £8,000 for the casualties, so outraged were they at the scale of the attack.

**Headlines from the *Caterham Times* of Friday 29th August 1975.**

The local press records the tragic incident at Caterham. Photographer Ron Poore of Banstead Road, Caterham, was one of the first at the scene.

The *Caterham Times* newspaper headlines on 29th August 1975, after the bombing.

*Many fires in the hot weather*

# Caterham in the 1975 summer

Life had to go on despite the shock of the bombing at the Caterham Arms on 27th August 1975. In the summer of that year, Caterham and Warlingham people were having a heated battle with the county council over plans to retain the gipsy site at Tupwood Lane for a further three years.

Councillor Nigel Stanners urged people to sign a petition against the plan.

A Warlingham man died at the British Industrial Sands lake in Merstham, when his dredger capsized in early August.

The hot weather led to several fires in the countryside. Fifteen horses were led to safety from the Kingswood Lane stables after 130 tons of hay went up in flames on 6th August. Firemen working to rule at Sanderstead Fire Station did not attend the blaze, and the stable owners felt that two children's lives had been put at risk as a result. A week later the work to rule was called off.

Police went in hot pursuit of a Triumph 2000 containing three youths and a girl, when it failed to stop in Limpsfield Road. The chase ended at Streatham, where the Triumph crashed and two youths ran off, but were later arrested.

A shortage of organizers put the Caterham Carnival in jeopardy. The popular event drew crowds of up to 8,000 people in the Seventies.

Threats to axe the 440 bus service between Caterham and Woldingham also caused alarm, but not as much as at Whyteleafe where, on 19th August, a lorry carrying soil crashed into the offices of Residential and Industrial holdings Ltd, almost demolishing the premises. It was the second time in a year that the offices, in Godstone Road, had been severely damaged by skidding lorries.

There was a drama at Dene Field, Caterham, in September, when a light aircraft taking part in an aerial display at a summer fair lost power and nose-dived to the ground. Miraculously, nobody was hurt.

Plans to bulldoze the Valley Hotel in Station Avenue, Caterham and replace it with a supermarket, came under fire in September and the same month residents in Eldon Road claimed they saw a UFO. It had bright red and green lights and was rotating rapidly.

**The shattered windows of the Caterham Arms, where the disco was being held.**

**Cracked earth at East Surrey Water's reservoir at Bough Beech, near Edenbridge in late August 1976.**

*On 18th June 1972, a BEA Trident One jet plane, callsign Papa India, fell from the sky into a field on the outskirts of Staines, resulting in the deaths of all 118 people on board. Apart from Lockerbie, it remains the worst air crash to have occurred in Britain. Barry Dix who, as a young reporter working for the airport press agency, was the first journalist to be informed of the crash, recalls the events of that dreadful Sunday afternoon.*

Headlines in the *Daily Express*, 19th June 1972.

It is not too difficult to pick out people who are strangers to Staines. They are the ones who look up, with a wide-eyed combination of wonderment and consternation, every time a jet aircraft whines over.

The rest of us, who live and work in this noise-blighted town have become so accustomed to the procession of Boeings and Airbuses passing above, that we rarely give them a second glance.

Events of 1972, however, have ensured that, whether we admit it or not, we often listen subconsciously until the roar of the engines fades into the distance.

The Staines air crash disaster was the nightmare that Staines people had feared for years and only by the narrowest of margins was it prevented from being an even more horrendous tragedy. A few more seconds in the air and the Trident would have plummeted onto the residential area to the south of the High Street.

Even now, Staines people who were involved in the rescue attempts are extremely reluctant to talk about the appalling scenes they witnessed on that dismal, wet afternoon in what had been a peaceful little corner on the edge of town.

The Trident hit the town only yards from Staines bypass, a mere three minutes after taking off en route to Brussels.

An airline strike had caused the cancellation of flights to Europe and many passengers had transferred to BEA from other carriers. When the jet hurtled along Heathrow's northern runway, every seat was occupied. Air Traffic Control gave the go-ahead for the three-engined Trident to climb and turn to the south, but within seconds, with sirens blaring in the cockpit, the plane went into a stall, from which it was impossible to recover. At the public inquiry a few months later, experts unravelled the sequence of events which had led to the

A *Daily Express* map of the crash site, indicating Egham nearby and the Crooked Billet roundabout.

crash.

Numerous contributory factors emerged, many of them involving the jet's Captain, Stanley Key, and the attitude of other BEA crews to the stance he had taken during a long-running dispute with management.

It emerged that Captain Key had possibly suffered a heart attack as the Trident became airborne. The most obvious reason for the disaster was that, for some reason, the "droops" on the leading edges of the Trident's wings, were retracted prematurely, causing the jet to stall.

Horrified motorists, driving home through the drizzle from abandoned Sunday outings, watched the Trident skim across the bypass and crash into

*Deaths of 118 people as jet plane plunges to ground*

# Staines air crash, 1972

**Part of the wreckage of the BEA Trident One jet after it crashed near Staines and Egham .**

the field close to where the old Staines Linoleum factory had been.

The jet hit the ground at 5.11pm. At the time I was on duty in the airport press agency newsroom and received a call from the *Daily Mail*'s news-desk, checking on a crash report. Feeling sure it was another false alarm — we had plenty of those — I got through to a contact at Heathrow Police Station, to be told: "Yes, it's a BEA Trident. It's come down near Staines and broken its back in two places."

Agency photographer Dave Barrett had listened in on another 'phone as I made the call. We looked at each other in utter disbelief. Until then I never believed a person's complexion could go grey.

It was not until 4am the following day that the telephones finally stopped ringing. Over the pre-vious few hours my colleagues and I had found ourselves dealing with publications from all over the world and even speaking on American radio.

Only one passenger survived, to be taken to hospital, but he died soon after arrival.

The impact of the crash had caused an explosion, which ripped the plane's tailplane off, intact. The sight of that predominantly blue piece of fuselage, with the airline's familiar half-Union Jack emblem, resting obscenely behind the rest of the Trident, will never leave those of us who saw it.

The field has remained unbuilt-on, unlike much of the surrounding land.

Suggestions have been made over the years that some sort of memorial should be put up to those who died, but nothing has ever come of the idea.

# Molesey girl in hot pants

Go-go dancers, electronic light shows and pop groups were provided, in 1970-1 by amongst others, the Mockingbird Discotheques run by Mr P.R. Crown of Crown's House Hotel and Restaurant, West Byfleet. Jean Walsh, left, and Shirley Coleman, right, were regular members of the discotheque team. Nearby, at Sheerwater, was the family home of Status Quo's Rick Parfitt, born at Church Street, Woking, in 1948.

In the early Seventies, hotpants and mini-skirts came into fashion. Here, brunette Laura Beaumont, aged 18, showed off her hot pants in front of 1971 discotheque equipment. Laura was managed by EPI music services in Station Road, Addlestone. She lived in a luxurious houseboat at Taggs Island, East Molesey and appeared on TV, playing Teresa Barton in the BBC's Doctors series. She also took part in various films including Chitty Chitty Bang Bang and featured in television advertisements for Danish bacon and Watney's beer. Her brother, Rick, nine, was also in showbiz and had a pop record out called Never Changes.

# Radio Jackie up a tree

Pirate pop music station, Radio Jackie, thrived in the Seventies. It broadcast from fields near Beverley School, New Malden, and from Epsom Downs at a spot behind the waterworks and close to the Derby Arms pub, in spite of efforts by the Post Office to close it down.

Other sites used included The Cock, at Headley, Sydenham Hill and the grounds of Tadworth Court Hospital, where an FM transmitting aerial was fixed to a tall fir tree. DJ, Mark Ellis, later recalled: "At Tadworth Court there was a cable coming down the tree, with a plug hanging down 20 feet above the ground."

Hospital staff did not know the grounds were being used for an illegal transmitting station, and one which was enjoyed by many Surrey listeners.

## YOUNG PUNK

Teenager, Bruce Whiting, whose stamping ground in 1979 was Woking and Guildford, was influenced by the emerging punk scene which was promoted by bands such as The Damned, from Croydon.

The foundations of the Woking Co-op superstore, which, in the 1980s, became Toys R Us. The Co-op spent years waiting for planning permission to build its new store. Twelve months after opening for business, it closed down. The swimming pool can be seen in the background. This was later demolished.

*Changed beyond recognition*

# Woking and the bulldozers

Woking changed beyond recognition in the Seventies. A blitz by bulldozers buried the past and made way for the new, as ambitious plans for the town centre came to fruition. However, parts of the new centre, with its typical Seventies architecture, were to last for only a few years. A bigger and better plan for Woking, involving the construction of The Peacocks Centre, had reached the drawing board by the following decade. A number of Seventies' buildings, such as the library, swimming pool and centre halls, were to face an untimely death.

The Atalanta dance hall, which saw the Rolling Stones perform there in the Sixties, was demolished in June 1972. Goldsworth Park housing estate was constructed in the 1970s and out in the villages Knaphill's Anchor Parade was built and at West Byfleet, Sheer House, Woolworth's and

Boots went up together with a new library, taking on an unusual octagonal shape.

A cinema was still open in Woking town and discotheques were held in the centre halls. Pupils utilized modern, new school buildings which had recently been opened. One of these was St. John the Baptist Roman Catholic Secondary School, whose first academic year was in 1970. Mr. Brian McCarthey was headmaster. Youngsters, as is often the case, complained of a lack of facilities and moaned that the new town was catering for the older generation. The Atalanta was supposed to be replaced with a new dance hall above Richard Shops and Clark's Shoes, in the new shopping centre which was later to be renamed Wolsey Place.

The modern shopping centre housed the largest Boots in the county, plus other anchor stores such

**Woking's Odeon cinema and a new-style 298 National bus. The Odeon started its life as a music hall called the Woking Palace Theatre. It later became the Astoria and then the Odeon. It was closed, and pulled down, at the end of the Seventies. The cinema stood on the corner of Duke Street and Broadway, Woking. New offices were constructed on the site.**

as Sainsbury's, Macfisheries, W.H.Smith and Robert Dyas.

Fine Fare was built in the Seventies and this store closed off the end of Commercial Road at the point where The Planets entertainment centre was built.

New office blocks in the town included Crown House, occupied by Crown Life Insurance, which in the early 1990s moved to Telford, Shropshire. The British American Tobacco Company occupied the speculative office development above "Wolsey Place' as it became christened. At that time Wolsey Walk was not covered and was a draughty place for shoppers as it often became a wind tunnel as air whistled round the towering offices above.

The town market moved to outside the post office, in the 1970s, from Goldsworth Road.

One notorious landmark, now disappeared, was the 'bridge of sighs.' This pedestrian footbridge linked Market Square with Goldsworth Road,

crossing the Victoria Way which, in the 1970s, was open to traffic. Victoria Way became the Woking town centre bypass, from Brock House to the roundabout, around the swimming pool and on to 'Co-op corner.'

The Centre Pool was opened in 1975 and was a family swimming pool with a learner pool for beginners. The main bath had a diving board. Discotheques used to be held in a vacant space under the the swimming pool level. The Centre Pool was demolished in the early 1990s, to make way for the building of the huge Peacocks shopping mall.

Today's modern library is next to the Peacocks, but in the 1970s it occupied another building on the site. The only civic building left standing, from those which were constructed in the 1970s, is the Rhoda McGaw theatre. It was carefully sheltered from the remaining Peacocks development and survived to become an integral part of The Peacocks arts and entertainments area.

The Chertsey Road Service Station at Woking, in about 1974. Brook House, to be used by a variety of firms, is in the background. When the garage site was sold for redevelopment, the business moved to Goldsworth Road but, confusingly, retained its former name. The garage was a Triumph dealer and issued Green Shield trading stamps.

Building work in Commercial Road, Woking, in May 1974. The premises on the far left survived the bulldozer for decades afterwards, and in the Nineties was used by Halfords motor accessories store. On the right of it was part of Gammons store and the other building, a few doors along and behind the scaffolding, was also a section of Gammons. Later this site became the home of the British Home Stores. In the distance can be seen Wearing's, the chemist's and the shops of Commercial Road. Here stood, firstly Fine Fare, then, when it closed, Gateway. Gateway, in turn, became Asda and latterly the Planets entertainment area.

Robinson's department store, Woking, on the left, was later occupied by McDonald's burger restaurant. Housed within the Robinson's building, too, was Pocock's the tobacconist, seen on the ground floor. Being built next to it in the Seventies, was a shops and offices extension to Robinson's. This site was occupied from 1895 to the late 1940s, by the Woking Post Office. Robinson's said, at the time, that Woking shoppers were not used to climbing stairs, so they wanted their shopping area to be mostly on the ground floor.

Victoria Way, Woking, with Brook House office block in the background. This is one of the few sites in the town which has not changed dramatically in two decades. The buildings on the right have gone and offices have been built to replace them. Note the RACS (Royal Arsenal Co-operative Society) van. This picture was taken on 15th May, 1974. More recently Brook House was used by several companies, including Appletise and Victoria Wine.

A number 29 bus, destined for Lightwater, near Camberley, makes its way along The Broadway, Woking, in 1971. Its route included Stoke, Jacob's Well, Sutton Green, Mayford and the Barnsbury estate.

A 1972 picture of Vale Farm Road, Woking. This terrace was in a derelict state and Woking Council spent a lot of money restoring the homes to make them habitable. Fifteen years later they were demolished. In 1995 the site had still not been built upon.

Christ Church and Church Path, in the mid-Seventies, with major work beginning on a new Woking town centre. The big, high-rise block in the background is Albion House, constructed in the early 1960s, which was the first office and shop development in Woking.

This was Church Street, Woking, in 1974. On the far right, work is under way on the new library — to be razed some 15 years later. In the middle, above the road, is the Marks and Spencer car park. The old exit was underneath the car park and emerged in Church Street. Woking Market was to move, in the 1990s, to a site shown in the central area of this photograph.

Some of the first shops to open in the Wolsey Place (Commercial Way, previously Commercial Road) centre. The stores included Peter Lord shoe shop. One unit, on the left, announces 'opening shortly,' and became Richard Shops, which continued to trade there well into the Nineties. Hepworth's men's clothes shop, took a unit on the right of Peter Lord's.

Commercial Road (later Commercial Way), with the new shops well under way in 1974-75. The premises above Peter Lord and Richard Shops, were earmarked to be a new ballroom to replace the Atalanta. This did not materialize due to disputes over the alleged high rents which were demanded.

This Woking Central Library no longer exists. Opened in 1975, it was pulled down just 15 years later. In April, 1975, the war memorial was moved just a few yards - at great expense.

The Co-op, in Percy Street, after it closed in the Seventies. Various traders took over the premises for a time including one who sold roller skates.

The building of Centre Halls in 1974. Fifteen years later they had been demolished.

Some of Woking Council's offices in the early Seventies. The council then had departments at York Road, Guildford Road and Mount Hermon Road. These were demolished in the 1980s.

The garage on the left is where Toys R Us was built in later years.

Church Street's Bond's Garage, called the Woking Garage, still standing on the corner of Clarence Avenue and Church Street, in the early '70s, but about to come down.

Looking down Church Street at the corner of Bath Road. Christ Church Hall is on the right with a car park in front. Winter's hardware shop is on the left. A few yards up was W.G. Trendell's, a furnisher's. The Aga shop, later to move to Cherry Street, is down the road on the left.

Bath Road with the Atalanta dance hall on the far right and Commercial Road shops on the left. Lying derelict is the YMCA building. This photograph was taken c.1972.

The 'Bridge of Sighs,' pedestrian footbridge in Victoria Way, Woking, in May 1974. It was called by this name because people moaned when crossing it.

Woking Centre Pool in May 1974. It was demolished about 16 years later to make way for the Peacocks Shopping Centre, and was replaced by a new swimming pool in Woking Park.

Victoria Way, Woking, with the Centre Hall building work on the left. The sign in the front of this derelict land says: "Site for proposed divisional police headquarters and magistrates court." This did not materialize. The site remained empty until The Peacocks was built and opened in 1992.

A site for development, looking towards Clarence Avenue and West Street, Woking, in the early 1970s. Boots was built in the vicinity.

Mac market was one of the main stores in the new Seventies Woking town centre, which later collectively became known as Wolsey Place. The shop unit later became Burton's and Dixon's. In this photograph taken in 1975, Saturday girl, Crishna Simmons poses next to a poster advertising PG Tips Tea, for 9p a quarter. When Crishna grew up she became a library manager at Woking in the Nineties.

# Surrey's topless disc jockey

**Mara O' Donnel , minus a few items of apparel, at the disco turntable in 1970.**

In 1970, Addlestone had its own topless DJ, Mara O'Donnel. The Review magazine, at Woking, carried an article about her: "She is a dark-haired, 19-year-old. When Mara starts to introduce the discs, wives and girlfriends are forgotten by their partners, who look, wide-eyed, at the only topless DJ in the country.

"Mara, however, appears to be completely unmoved by the smiling faces and scores of male eyes focussed upon her." Mara was the DJ of the Oakley-Cohen discotheque and lightshow which was featured at the February Decimalisation Rag Week at Southampton University.

The entertainment agency, run by Rodney Oakley of Row Town, Addlestone, and Nick Cohen, of Oatlands Drive, Weybridge, included a £250,000 IBM computer, programmed to make moving linear light patterns which are then filmed. Their disco unit, built by Nick Cohen, incorporated "6,000 watts of pulsed light, stroboscopic effects, computer memory banks and control panels."

It cost £3,000 to build and was said to be one of the most powerful in the U.K.

**On the left is Chertsey Road, with the station in the far distance. The whole of the foreground, with shops such as J.H. Barrenger's leatherwear, Belfast Linen Warehouse and John's gent's hairdresser, which is on the right, were to disappear. Owen's wool shop also vanished. The whole of this area became the Fine Fare supermarket, well into the Seventies.**

## Pop stars in Surrey

# Keith Moon moves to Chertsey

Keith Moon, one of rock music's most flamboyant characters and drummer with The Who, lived near Chertsey in the early Seventies. The zany musician, renowned for his wild behaviour, bought Tara House, St. Ann's Hill, for £60,000 in 1970.

A reporter for the *Woking Review* paid him a visit in the early autumn of 1971 and noted: "Dressed in cord shirt and jeans — he appeared relaxed amid the activity of assorted workmen making alterations to his luxurious house." He added: "The country life seems to be suited to his tastes and, surrounded by innumerable cats and dogs, he looks to be in his element."

**Keith Moon pictured at the Chertsey Show, c. 1971.**

The reporter observed that Beatles' songs were playing from a tape recorder in the house, which was designed with pyramid-shaped roofs. One of the rooms had been converted into a studio.

The star had become a 'local' at his nearby pub and described his neighbours as "incredible," but he was more unbelievable. His Rolls Royce ended up in the lake outside his home. Kevin Godley, of 10cc, bought it from him in 1974.

In September 1973, Bad Company held their first rehearsals at Albury Village Hall. Camberley's local band, The Members, shot to fame with the hit "The Sound of the Suburbs" in 1979. The Stranglers, formerly the Guildford Stranglers, lived in Chiddingfold and the Moody Blues' singer, Ray Thomas, bought a palatial house in Cobham for £16,000 in June 1970.

The Greyhound pub in Park Lane, Croydon, had top names playing there. These included Genesis and David Bowie, who is said to have offered his song "All the Young Dudes" to an up-and-coming Mott the Hoople. They took up his offer, following their meeting at The Greyhound and became famous. It was also at this pub that ELO gave their debut show. At Fairfield Halls, Croydon, Captain Sensible was a toilet cleaner in the early Seventies and Surrey-born Rat Scabies

was a porter. They decided to form The Damned in May 1976 and two months later supported the Sex Pistols at a London gig. Their first single, New Rosa, is regarded as the very first UK punk recording.

Stephen Stills lived at Elstead in the early Seventies in the "haunted" mansion previously owned by Peter Sellers and Ringo Starr.

At Ewell, the NESCOT college, in Reigate Road, was where Elvis Costello's 'pub' band, Flip City, played their final gig. They supported The Climax Blues Band in December 1975. Guildford was the home of progressive rock act Camel and Mungo Jerry's Ray Dorsett, who now lives in Farnham.

In September 1972, Ron Wood allegedly paid £140,000 for The Wick, on Richmond Hill.

David Bowie began his Ziggy Stardust tour at The Toby Jug, Tolworth, in February 1972. The Jam's Paul Weller, Paul Buckler and Bruce Foxton, were all educated at Sheerwater Comprehensive School, all leaving c. 1970-71. Paul Weller was the youngest of the three, by three years. He attended Maybury Primary School, Woking, and lived in Stanley Road, where the group used to rehearse. His home was later demolished and the site redeveloped. Weller's father, John, then managed the band.

Robin Gibb, of the Bee Gees, lived in the Surrey countryside 'near Esher' and is said to have once had a sighting of the infamous Surrey Puma. It was said that he called a London Zoo expert, to make plaster casts of the pawmarks in the mud.

Eric Clapton's mother lived in Ripley, Jonathan King and DJ Mike Reid all had Surrey connections for many years and the flat-capped Gilbert O'Sullivan resided on the St. George's Hill estate, near Weybridge, as did Cliff Richard.

Hot Chocolate's Errol Brown had a home on the Claremont side of Esher and was once a special guest at a fête in Claygate in 1977.

# An interview with The Police

**Band members of The Police group in 1978 signing a copy of Roxanne in a chance meeting with some Leatherhead teenagers in Kingston Road. From left to right: Stewart Copeland, Darren Walton, Don Woodham, Ian Allan and Sting.**

Leatherhead was an important place in the pop world during the Seventies, for it was here that The Police recorded their first album, Outlandos D'Amour, which spent 96 weeks in the charts and ensured that Sting and his musical friends were to be remembered for decades.

During one such visit, to Nigel Gray's Surrey Sound Studio, at 70, Kingston Road, the band were spotted in 1978 by some Leatherhead teenagers from the top of a bus.

Ian Allan, of Kingston Road, Leatherhead, then aged about 12, recalled: "We had been to Tower Records and had bought a copy of Roxanne. I was with my friends, Don Woodham and Darren Walton. We had been to Kingston, shopping, during the half-term holiday and were on a bus when we looked out and saw three members of The Police outside the studio next to the milk depot. We got off the bus quickly and ran up to them. Sting signed our copy of Roxanne and a Japanese photographer took our picture, which appeared in a fan magazine, called Police File. We were all very excited. They were very obliging."

## The Cure played on Earlswood Common

In the mid-Seventies, the earliest incarnation of international superstars, The Cure emerged from sleepy Horley. Just across the Surrey/Sussex border, in Crawley, an early line-up, at the time called The Easy Cure and featuring Robert Smith, Horley man Lol Tolhurst and Paul Thompson, played a local summer music festival on the green at Earlswood Common, near Redhill, opposite The Railway pub. Horley man Stuart Curran later recalled watching this gig as a young boy. He said: "They were quite good, very punky and stood out from the other bands, who were old rockers and hippies. Robert Smith was wearing a fake fur coat. They kept playing even though it began to rain." Among other bands at the festival were Lockjaw and Magazine Spies, from which The Cure recruited their bassist, Simon Gallup, in about 1979.

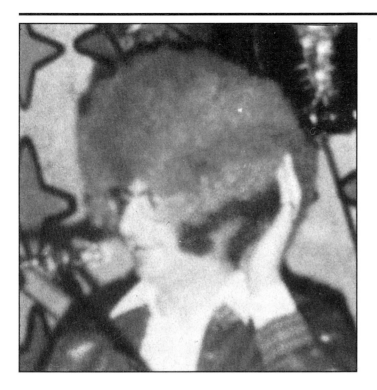

# A King's bid to become an MP

Pop star Jonathan King raised a few eyebrows when he stood in a parliamentary by-election in Epsom and Ewell on 27th April 1978.

The singer of the Sixties hit "Everyone's Gone to the Moon" toured the district in his limousine and on one occasion parked it outside the *Epsom and Ewell Herald*'s office in Upper High Street, announcing to the receptionist: "I'm Jonathan King and I'm standing for MP."

The result of the election was A.Hamilton (Conservative) 28,242; A. Mooney (Labour) 7,314: M. Anderson (Liberal) 5,673: J. King (Independent) 2,350; J. Sanger (National Front) 823.

The Conservative majority had been reduced by about 4,000 votes since the previous election, in October 1974. Jonathan King is pictured here at the Walton Hop disco at Walton on Thames in the 1970s.

## Fairfield Halls pop concerts 1973

| | |
|---|---|
| 28th January | Uriah Heep |
| 22nd February | Al Stewart |
| 26th February | Labi Siffre |
| 8th March | New World |
| 11th March | The Supremes |
| 8th April | Ten Years After |
| 3rd May | Groundhogs |
| 6th May | The New Seekers |
| 17th May | Focus |
| 20th May | Cilla Black |
| 27th May | Fleetwood Mac |
| 3rd June | Barclay James Harvest |
| 15th July | Procul Harum |
| 2nd September | Hawkwind |
| 4th September | Georgie Fame |
| 9th September | Family |
| 16th September | Argent |
| 7th October | The Kinks |
| 12th October | Don Maclean |
| 2nd November | The Four Tops |
| 9th November | Steeleye Span |
| 22nd November | Cliff Richard |
| 27th November | Al Stewart |
| 29th November | Billy Paul; O'Jays |
| 30th November | Richie Havens |
| 2nd December | Manfred Mann's Earthband |
| 7th December | Donovan |
| 16th December | Fairport Convention |

This garage in Woodbridge Road, Guildford, was making a larger-than-life offer on Green Shield Stamps in 1975.

#  Index to towns and villages

Skateboards were all the rage in Richmond in 1973.

# ✶ Index to towns and villages ✶

# Mark Davison

Mark has been fascinated by Surrey's history since he was a teenager, when he kept a daily diary of events in Hook and Kingston. In the late Seventies, after leaving school, he joined the *Kingston Borough News* and started up a district edition covering part of the Elmbridge villages of Thames Ditton, Long Ditton and Claygate. His newspaper career took him to the *Surrey Mirror* at Redhill and then to the *Banstead Herald* and the Oxted edition of the *Surrey Mirror*, before working for a year in Derbyshire. As well as contributing to the local history sections of the papers he has worked on, he has also written a popular weekly pop column. He currently works at the *Surrey Mirror*'s head office newsroom in Reigate. He now lives in Reigate and in recent years has run a weekly Motown music night in Dorking. Together with Ian Currie, he has written several books about the weather in Southern counties and a best-selling title, *Surrey In the Hurricane*. More recently, he co-wrote *Surrey In The Sixties*.

# Ian Currie

Ian lived in Wallington in the mid 1970s and took a particular interest in the great heatwave of 1976. He taught for 13 years at de Stafford School, Caterham, and in 1979 moved to Rickman Hill, Coulsdon. His interest in the weather has grown over the years and now he works full-time as a freelance forecaster and weather historian. Ian is a member of the Croydon Natural History and Scientific Society and is in charge of their weather section. He has many archives on well-known storms in the Seventies, including the snows of 1978-79 in the Winter of Discontent when there were numerous strikes around Surrey. He often gives illustrated talks on the weather to clubs and organisations in the South East and is keen to relate stories of Seventies' storms to his growing audiences. Ian has a regular weather column in the *Surrey Mirror* series, the *Dorking and Leatherhead Advertisers* and the *Sutton Herald* group. He is a daily forecaster on Radio Mercury and has a weekly slot on United Artists cable TV. He accurately predicted the Great Storm of 1987.

## Other titles by the same authors

**Surrey In the Sixties** (ISBN 0-9516710-4-9) PRICE £9.95 Published by Frosted Earth
**The Surrey Weather Book** (ISBN 0-9516710-3-0 Price £8.95 Published by Frosted Earth

*IN THE SAME SERIES:*
**Surrey Street, Croydon—100 years of market trading** by Vivien Lovett (ISBN 0-9516710-5-7)
**Red Sky At Night — Weather Sayings For All Seasons** (ISBN 0-9516710-2-2) Price £4.95
Published by Frosted Earth
**Surrey in the Hurricane** (ISBN 0-9513019-2-6) Price £7.50 Published by Froglets
**London's Hurricane** (ISBN 0-9513019-3-4) Price £7.95

Other books which the authors have co-written include historical county weather books pictorially recording the major floods, blizzards and heatwaves in Sussex, Kent, Berkshire, Hampshire, Norfolk & Suffolk and Essex. These are published by Froglets/Frosted Earth. Telephone 01737 554869 for enquiries or 01959 562972.